alvar aalto

alvar

göran
schildt

masterworks

aalto

universe

First published in the United States of America in 1998
by UNIVERSE PUBLISHING
A Division of Rizzoli International Publications, Inc.
300 Park Avenue South
New York, NY 10010

Revised edition of *Alvar Aalto: The Complete Catalogue of
Architecture, Design and Art* by Göran Schildt, first published
in the United States of America in 1994 by Rizzoli International
Publications, Inc.

Library of Congress Cataloging-in-Publication Data
Schildt, Göran.
  Alvar Aalto: masterworks / Göran Schildt.
     p.   cm.
ISBN 0-7893-0131-8 (pbk.)
   1. Aalto, Alvar, 1898–1976—Criticism and interpretation. 2.
Architecture, Modern—20th century. 3. Architect-designed decorative
arts—Finland. I. Aalto, Alvar, 1898–1976. II. Title.
NA 1455.F53A23715   1998
720'.92—dc21   98-10216

98 99 00 / 10 9 8 7 6 5 4 3 2 1

Translated by Timothy Binham
Design by John Klotnia
Printed in Italy

CONTENTS

Introduction

Michael Trencher

FINNISH ARCHITECT ALVAR AALTO inherited directly from his culture and family a value system that honored Western humanistic traditions stemming from the Renaissance and Classical antiquity while simultaneously maintaining a deep commitment to indigenous Finnish culture, with its devotion to nature. Aalto's father was a surveyor whose professional responsibilities stressed the proper management of the natural environment for human benefit. The younger Aalto's comprehensive understanding of the landscape, its measurement, description, and manipulation established the framework for his extraordinary skill at siting, landscaping, and contextually integrating his individual and clustered buildings. His intimate experience with the Finnish wilderness formed the basis for his sensibility for natural form, materials, and space.

After graduating from architectural school in Helsinki, Aalto returned to his central Finnish hometown of Jyväskylä, where he immediately opened an office. Known locally as the "Athens of Finland" because of its nationalistic roots, the town and its surrounding region became the context of Aalto's provincial period, during which he embraced an Italianate style filled with mannered details. These details broke down the formalism inherent in High Renaissance architecture and thus allowed the architecture of the newly independent Finnish nation to connect with the democratic ideals of Western humanism without the encumbrance of monumentality. Both the Jyväskylä Workers' Club and the Seinäjoki Defense Club Building are representative of this provincial style while integrating other essential Aaltonian characteristics: a manipulation of historical typology, an imaginative interpretation of program, references to contemporaneous models enlivened by a visual wit. As with many other Aalto buildings of the period, there are direct references to the formal, Classical, and mannered works of the leading Swedish architect Gunnar Asplund, who until his untimely death in 1940, remained Aalto's mentor. The Workers' Club established a formal paradigm—an object (assembly hall) within a frame (palazzo shell) adapted to a theater typology, the lobby between becoming a negative, exterior space. This formal idea became the model for all of Aalto's theaters, especially Essen Opera House, Finlandia Hall, and Seinäjoki Theater, although the morphology evolves to more complex non-Euclidean forms, and the resulting negative space becomes more fluid and organic.

At the end of the 1920s, after observing the decade-long international development of German Modernism and the growing influence of the Bauhaus at Dessau, Scandinavian architects—including Aalto and led by Asplund—enthusiastically adopted the Modernist agenda. After moving his office and young family to Turku, Aalto won a competition for Paimio Sanatorium, his design of which demonstrated his mastery of the new style. Encouraged by his new friend, Laszlo Moholy-Nagy of the Bauhaus, Aalto enriched the language of Modernism with a celebration of organic planning, programming, and detailing. Recognizing that the cure of TB required sunlight, fresh air, and exercise, Aalto and his design team maximized the patients' exposure to natural light, oriented common areas to optimal exposures, and elongated the circulation to enhance patient movement. He scrutinized the detailing of lighting fixtures, furniture, hardware, and interiors, resulting in extraordinary inventions dedicated to enhancing the recuperation of the patient in a humanistic, physiological, and psychologically appropriate manner.

In the 1930s Aalto continued this evolutionary redefinition of the International style with amazing self-confidence, so that by the end of the decade he had completely transformed it into what may be called Organic Modernism. In the Paris World's Fair Finnish Pavilion, Aalto made wood the central theme by integrating the natural treescape into the courtyards, blurring interior spatial definition with use of wooden screens, wrapping the main hall with a wooden curtain wall, and juxtaposing primitive clustered columns with sophisticated industrial posts.

The Villa Mairea, also of the 1930s, employs the Cubist collage technique to combine overlapping layers of materials, colors, textures, and forms that allude simultaneously to historical and modern references, natural and industrial elements. The main room is simultaneously a traditional Finnish farm living room, a "tupa" as at Eliel Saarinen's 1902 home at Hvitträsk, a Japanese pavilion, a Miesian universal space, and a natural forest. The ensemble tells a sequential narrative of the evolution of the house and its modern, organic, and cultural synthesis into a contemporary paradigm, a poetic antiphonal to Le Corbusier's Villa Savoye, Mies van der Rohe's Tugendhat House, and Frank Lloyd Wright's Fallingwater.

Through the war years Aalto adapted his extensive prewar developments in industrialized housing to the crisis of refugee settlements. These studies led to his postwar appointment to the faculty of the Massachusetts Institute of Technology in Cambridge, where in 1946 he received a commission for a large dormitory. In Baker House, Aalto further developed major formal, typological, and programmatic themes. Inverting Le Corbusier's group-residential paradigm of the Swiss Pavilion, Aalto transformed the residential block into a roughly hewn, dynamic curve that opposes the Classical atrium-centered dining hall. Derived directly from his 1930s abstract reliefs that in turn generated from his furniture design, the transformation of the wave ("aalto" in Finnish) into architectural form is an extension of the organic formal language used internally at the internationally celebrated New York World's Fair Pavilion.

The death of Aalto's first wife and professional colleague, Aino Marsio, in 1949 interrupted the completion of the dormitory and set the tone for a conservative and retrospective period in his work best represented by the court-centered town hall at Säynätsalo. Simultaneously antique, Italianate, and reminiscent of traditional Finnish farms, the court becomes a humanistic exterior room for community gatherings in sharp contrast to the elevated cubic town hall chamber.

In other designs of the early 1950s, the formal vocabulary remains traditionally Euclidean and court-centered. The National Pensions Institute in Helsinki develops the court theme internally and externally, creating a worker's paradise that serves the community and the employees simultaneously. Raised above street level on granite outcroppings and on an underground circulation system, the gym, library, and dining hall define an exterior space linked to the surrounding community. In addition to the formal and programmatic invention evident in the building, the interiors demonstrate a remarkable burst of creativity in the development of new skylight forms, lighting fixtures, furniture, wall cladding, and window detailing. This new explosion of creative work that extends through the early 1960s coincides with Aalto's marriage, in 1952, to a young architect in his office, Elissa Mäkiniemi.

Near the end of the 1950s, Aalto's exploration of new forms for cultural typologies reached its most creative period. His most extraordinary work, the Church of the Three Crosses at Vuoksenniska, responds to Le Corbusier's poetic and enigmatic structure, Ronchamp. Aalto transforms the nave church into a series of ascending waves that billow up and out, forming a tripartite integration of sacred and profane, of holy ritual and secular activities.

At the same time, Aalto gained several significant commissions in Germany. In the ongoing reconstruction after World War II, Aalto could participate in reshaping the modern world by correcting the anti-humanistic tendencies of political dogmatism of left and right, rejoining Western cultural traditions, and mediating the schism between industrialism and naturalism. At Bremen, in a new quarter of socialized housing dedicated to the survivors of the war, Aalto was asked to build a humanistic tower as a symbol of the new society. In a remarkable synthesis, he integrated three of his major motifs: the undulating curve, the irregular fan or radiant plan, and the stepped plane.

The crystalization of this new organic composite form marks the beginning of Aalto's mature period, which reached its purest form in the competition design for the Essen Opera House of 1959. Here the theater typology, previously articulated at the Jyväskylä Workers' Club, of an assembly hall within a simple rectilinear frame, has been transformed from traditional geometry into an organic composition, with the foyer space becoming an interior canyon.

It is Seinäjoki, the small Finnish city of Aalto's youth, that is enriched by the formal modulations of his mature period. In Aalto's only completely manifested urban design, the town center becomes the synthesis of antique acropolis and Italian hilltown. Although located on the flat plains of western Finland, the design follows the ancient models by defining an irregular yet linear pedestrian spine by the careful placement of discrete programmatic units—church, town hall, library, and theater. Each has a distinct definition related to its typology and the newly enriched formal vocabulary.

By the end of Aalto's long, fruitful career, his continuous morphological explorations had produced a body of work that freed future generations of designers and architects from the stylistic and sterile constraints of Modernism's rigid formulation. Moreover, his enrichment and broadening of material vocabulary combined with exemplary manipulations of natural light reinforced the human centeredness of his vision. His respect for history and context, as opposed to revolutionary dogmatism, places him in the mainstream of Western culture.

Seinäjoki Defense Corps Building 1924

IN BUILDINGS INTENDED for wholly voluntary cultural activities—whether idealistic, amateur, or professional—we find a lively and spontaneous commitment on Aalto's part. His enthusiasm for this field of planning was so great that more than once he designed cultural centers and club buildings unasked and unpaid.

Aalto designed many buildings for defense corps, the armed home guard that flourished in Finland between the wars. Training in the use of arms was only one of the tasks assumed by the defense corps, which had patriotism in the broadest sense of the word as its main aim. Aalto, whose father was head of a local defense corps, took a favorable view of the movement's main purpose—safeguarding Finnish independence and national identity—whereas he was highly critical of its dogmatism and disciplinary tendencies.

From the 1920s on, a large number of buildings for local defense corps went up in Finland. Sometimes the defense corps shared the space with other organizations or took up quarters in multipurpose buildings; just as often, however, they had buildings exclusively their own. Both types of buildings are represented in Aalto's canon. Thus, the Jyväskylä Defense Corps Building was multipurpose, whereas the one in Jalasjärvi was used by the defense corps alone. The forceful architecture of these buildings frequently made them stand out. During the 1920s, they were mostly in Classicist style, but in the 1930s several were characterized by far-reaching Functionalism. The defense corps were forced to disband after the conclusion of peace in 1944, whereupon their buildings were taken over mostly by local cultural organizations.

It is interesting to note that while working on defense corps buildings, Aalto also

designed buildings for left-wing workers' associations, such as the "House of the People" (Workers' Club) in Jyväskylä (page 16); the "House of Culture" in Helsinki (page 104) was actually commissioned by the Finnish Communist Party. Nor was he loath to place his skills at the disposal of mainstream Christian and sectarian societies. The principle of voluntary participation by the general public in these organizations was sacred to Aalto. He considered that they were all useful to society and enriched the country's cultural life.

Aalto designed this building in 1924, and it was completed in 1929. The client was the Southern Ostrobothnia Defense Corps, which used the three-story building with mixed functions as its headquarters. The semi-subterranean ground floor, which contains a circular assembly hall, foyer, and

cloakroom, is built of stone; the office level and the residential story (at the top with its own access stairs) are of wood. The unusual stair hall, facade pilasters, and assembly hall painted in Pompeiian style make this one of the chief works of Aalto's Neoclassical period. Aalto originally designed a loggialike staircase for the end entrance, similar to that shown in the plan for the Lahtinen House, but it was not built.

Together with the main building, a separate outbuilding was designed and erected on the other side of the courtyard, which was intended as a drill and parade ground. The ground floor of this two-story building of rendered brick contains a garage, guardhouse, arms depot, sauna, and laundry; there are four small apartments in the upper story. An unusual stair arrangement on both sides of the arched entrance provides separate access to most of the various facilities.

Jyväskylä Workers' Club

1924–25

DESIGNED IN 1924 for the Jyväskylä worker's association and erected that and the following year, this building marked Aalto's breakthrough. The earliest sketches show a large, colonnaded forecourt that was not built. The largely windowless upper floor contained an auditorium used for political assemblies and as a theater with stage, parterre, balconies, and foyer. These facilities were used by the workers' theater and later by the city theater. A monumental staircase led from the foyer down to the lower level, which was basically a glazed colonnade containing a restaurant, two cafe rooms, and the entrance hall to the theater. Aalto designed the furniture, light fixtures, and fittings specially. The theater moved out in the 1970s, and the restaurant and cafes were converted into shops. The building's degradation has, however, recently been halted: the theater has been restored as a meeting hall and the old cafe rooms now house a restaurant.

Paimio Tuberculosis Sanatorium 1929

THE 1920S AND '30S were a time of tremendous progress in Finnish health care. Under the supervision of the National Board of Health, numerous central and regional hospitals were built. A network of tuberculosis sanatoria and mental institutions sprang up throughout the country. Usually the clients were towns, municipalities, and municipal associations.

Aalto took an early interest in this type of institutional architecture from the 1920s on. His municipal hospital in Alajärvi and old people's home in Säynätsalo represented the kind of small-scale institutions built by rural municipalities.

The fight against tuberculosis in the 1920s and '30s proved gratifyingly successful. The advance of the feared disease was gradually brought to a halt through the construction of functional sanatoria. Jussi Paatela, sometimes in collaboration with his brother Toivo, was the architect of most of the major new hospitals in Finland as a result of numerous competition victories. Aalto won first prize in only one hospital competition, that of the Paimio Sanatorium, which was the very building that catapulted him into the international architectural elite. In this work, Aalto combined impulses from Le Corbusier and Walter Gropius with the ideas of the Dutch architect Johannes Duiker to produce a design unmistakably his own. The standard Functionalist call for light, air, and sunshine was particularly relevant to the ideas of the period on the care of TB patients.

Aalto thought of health care as a joint effort by physicians and architects, both contributing directly to the cure. This attitude was illustrated especially clearly in the Paimio Sanatorium design, in which every architectural detail had a clinical function and formed part of

the treatment. Thus his justification for the renowned Paimio chair (see page 222) was not based on considerations of industrial production or requirements of aesthetic form: in his mind, the angle of its seat was supposed to ease the patients' breathing.

The highly rationalized and technological orientation of modern health care, however, made it difficult for Aalto to reconcile medical and nature-related goals convincingly, especially in designing ordinary hospitals. He took part in several hospital design competitions, but had no more successes after the Paimio victory.

The Paimio competition was announced in November 1928, with January 31, 1929, as the deadline. Aalto's winning entry had the drawing of an L-shaped window as its motto. He divided the functions among a number of freely combined building volumes. A dominant patients' wing with a slightly angled open-air ward facing south communicates with a central entrance section containing the stairs and elevators. This part connects with a lower wing placed at an angle, containing the canteen, kitchen, and social facilities, beyond which another obliquely placed service wing connects with the whole. For the competition entry, Aalto borrowed the L-shaped windows of the patients' rooms from André Lurçat, but at the construction stage these were replaced for practical reasons with conventional windows. Increased space requirements had the result that the building (erected 1929–32) ultimately became three stories higher than in the original plan, accentuating the monumental impression. The pantiled monopitch roof of the

24 PAIMIO TUBERCULOSIS SANATORIUM/1929

competition entry was replaced with a flat Rationalist roof both for the main building and the surrounding staff housing. The complex also included a greenhouse and a mortuary of the same type as in the Jyväskylä funeral chapel design. As a result of Finland's success in fighting tuberculosis, Paimio Sanatorium was later converted into an ordinary hospital, resulting in extensive alterations and new construction.

Describing the Paimio Sanatorium in a lecture in Italy (1956), Aalto said: "The main purpose of the building is to function as a medical instrument"; in this, "one of the basic prerequisites for healing is to provide complete peace. [...] The room design is determined by the depleted strength of the patient, reclining in his bed. The color of the ceiling is chosen for quietness, the light sources are outside the patient's field of vision, the heating is oriented towards the patient's feet, and the water runs soundlessly from the taps to make sure that no patient disturbs his neighbor" (text in the Aalto archives).

Viipuri City Library

1933

LIBRARIES WERE A LEITMOTIF in Aalto's oeuvre, a theme to which he returned time and again throughout his life. His library plans thus provide a coherent summary of his development.

His first significant effort in the field was the library wing included in his 1923 competition entry for the Finnish Parliament House. In it Aalto tried out a highly original cross between a cubicized Classical theater cavea and an open-shelf system directly accessible to the public. This motif was transformed in the 1927 competition entry for the Viipuri City Library into his first sunken "book pit," which reappeared in modified form in most of his later library designs. The book pit suggestively alludes to literature as man's underlying spiritual foundation; librarians, however, have criticized it as unfunctional and laborious.

Aalto's Classicist competition design of the Viipuri Library still relied on the example of Gunnar Asplund, but the final plan of 1933 introduced a series of functional "inventions" in the plan itself, while stylistically pointing to Walter Gropius and Le Corbusier. Viipuri Library was Finland's first Functionalist library building.

In his next competition design, the 1937 entry for an annex to the Helsinki University Library, Aalto confirmed his opposition—already evident in the Viipuri Library auditorium—to the rigidity and geometric formality of Rationalism. In the Jyväskylä University library from 1953–55, he had the stacks rise, stairlike, from the lending counter at the bottom level; this complicated solution, however, unfavorably affected the building's height. When designing the Seinäjoki City Library (page 180) in 1958, Aalto discovered a solution on which he based most of his later library plans: a fan arrangement of the book collection, placed like an annex at the long end of

MAIN ENTRANCE

a rectangular building volume containing the offices and other subsidiary functions. This plan solution could be combined with smaller book pits, as in the Rovaniemi City Library (page 188), or it could take the form of concentric, theaterlike terraces on a sloping site, as in the Mount Angel Library in Oregon (page 210).

From the 1950s on, Aalto's efforts to bestow on his cultural buildings a free-form, sculptural overall impact by having the exterior mirror the asymmetry of the interior (as in the Helsinki House of Culture, page 104) are reflected in some of his library designs, such as the 1966 plan for Kokkola Library.

For a 1927 competition to design the Viipuri City Library Aalto designed the winning entry, but reworked it repeatedly before it was built. After the City Council decided on the new placing of the library in Torkkeli park in autumn 1933, Aalto drafted the final version and signed the drawings in December 1933. Construction got under way in 1934, and the library was inaugurated on October 13, 1935. As planned earlier, the facades were finished with white rendering in Le Corbusier style, but the collagelike overlapping of building volumes and the new location called for a redisposition of rooms. The staircase can be seen through a glass wall from the entrance hall, which merges with a long auditorium; the children's library, lending room, reading rooms, and basement stacks are more tightly integrated into the main volume. The original Asplund-style "book pit" still forms the main entrance to the lending room and its centrally placed

"librarian's watchtower." Aalto reverted to his original idea of top-lighting for the lending and reading rooms, though this time he solved the problems of winter snow and direct sunlight with rows of round "barrel skylights" that rise above the roof surface (an idea used previously by Aalto for some basement storerooms in the Turun Sanomat building). This meant deleting the rooftop garden. Other important innovations included a generous use of light, unpainted wood panelling, irregular serpentine lines in the interiors, and specially designed, functional light fixtures. To make up for the auditorium's acoustically unfavorable elongated shape, Aalto developed the acoustic ceiling design of his 1930 competition entry for Tehtaanpuisto Church, using an apparently free—but in fact quite uniform—undulating form. The convincing overall grasp, the density of ideas, and the care taken with every detail guarantee the Viipuri Library pride of place in Aalto's prewar output.

In an English manuscript in the Aalto archives, Aalto explains his solutions to the problems of lighting and acoustics in the Viipuri Library: "The ceiling (of the reading rooms and lending room) has 57 round, conical openings, 1.8 meters in diameter, which function as skylights. The principle is as follows: the depth of the cones ensures that no light rays can penetrate at an angle of 52° or less. Thus the lighting is indirect all year round. This achieves two goals: first, the books are protected from direct sunlight, and second, the reader is not disturbed by shadows or sharp light, whatever his position in relation to the book. The inner surfaces of the cones reflect daylight in such a way that the rays from each spread like a diffuse cluster over a large floor surface. Every seat in the reading room, receiving light from several cones, is thus bathed in a composite light.

"The ceiling of the auditorium consists of joined wooden slats (with a total surface of 58 square meters), which disseminate sound, particularly speech at close quarters, in an acoustically advantageous way. Since debate is as important as lectures, audibility is not merely in one direction, as in concert halls. My acoustic construction is aimed at making every point in the auditorium equal as a transmitter and a receiver of words spoken at normal loudness over the floor. I consider acoustic problems to be primarily physiological and psychological, which is why they cannot be solved by purely mechanical means."

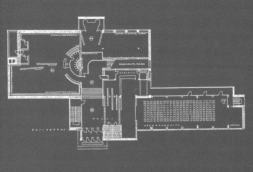

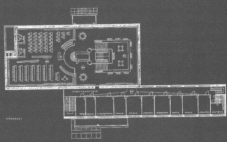

Sunila
Sulphate Pulp
Mill
1936

THE EXPANSION OF THE wood-processing industry in the 1920s and '30s transformed the Finnish landscape. Industrial communities rapidly developed into towns, usually dominated completely by one factory. The plans for these communities were drawn up and the production plants and housing built under company supervision. The business world thus frequently assumed duties that had traditionally fallen to the government—and do so again today. This was in fact essential in order to attract skilled labor. Company-run clubhouses, restaurants, hospitals, kindergartens, schools, fire stations, parks, etc., were built in many of these communities. Thus, the clients for the great variety of buildings designed by Aalto for industrial communities were always the companies that owned the local works.

In the 1920s, industrial estates were built to established patterns derived from old industrial communities. New housing types and a freer way of thinking took over in the 1930s. For Aalto, the key issue was to remain within financial and practical limits. He often had to be content with designing factories and workers' housing that were free from the worst ills of industrialism caused by unscrupulous speculation and indifference to the environment. To design a sober and practical building related in some way to its surroundings was an achievement in itself. Only occasionally did he have the opportunity to design overall environments which might serve as models. The first was in 1930, when he was commissioned to give the Toppila-Vaala pulp mill near Oulu its external form. The second came in 1936, when he was asked to draw up the master plan and detail plans of the Sunila pulp mill and housing area on unspoilt land near Kotka. Again in the early 1950s, designing the Summa paper mill and housing area and the Typpi Oy chemical plant near Oulu, he produced comprehensive plans that aspired to give rise to a truly acceptable industrial environment.

The most prominent aspect of Aalto's industrial architecture was that he strove to relate it to nature in various ways. This applies to the blending of buildings with the immediate environment as well as to the internal relations between building volumes, which he grouped organically, following nature's own example. Aalto was no opponent of technology; in fact he saw it as man's great opportunity to create bearable living conditions on earth. What he did oppose was an excessively narrow technology founded on short-term thinking, which shatters the all-embracing system of equilibrium on which life on earth is based. The specific problem and great task of our time, according to Aalto, is "the step by step transition of industrialism into what it is in any case destined to be some day—a harmonious factor of civilization."

Aalto's obsession with nature sometimes found unexpected outlets in his industrial architecture. Thus, when planning the Sunila mill complex, he wished to give every worker in the factory halls a window view of the surrounding forests and sea inlets. He refused to blast the cliff on which the Sunila mill stands because pulp manufacture, as he put it, "resembles slalom skiing: it zigzags downhill." The directors, who wished to remove the cliff in order to place the mill on level ground, gave in to Aalto's argument—to the present management's regret. During every renovation, the differences in elevation have turned out to complicate planning and impair efficiency. The attractive brick walls of the mill have proved less disruptive, though superfluous, as has the

SULPHATE WAREHOUSE, ROOF-BEARING
PARABOLIC WOODEN ARCHES

sulphate storehouse's load-bearing roof structure of organically shaped laminated wood. The question is whether these touches made the factory more "natural," better integrated into the totality of life. From the present-day perspective, Aalto's efforts to adapt industrialism to nature seem rather marginal. It is undeniable that people gladly accept the paper, energy, fertilizers, prefabricated housing, and many other products with which Aalto's pulp and paper mills, power plants, and house factories provide them; however, the real problems of air and water pollution, the seepage of artificial fertilizers into watercourses, the insufficiency of nonpolluting energy resources, and so forth, had not yet become acute and were therefore not apparent in Aalto's time. His contribution to a balanced environment was in fact woefully inadequate. It is also obvious that an effective solution to the problems of industrialism lies beyond the influence and scope of the individual architect. Thus the important point about Aalto's industrial architecture was that it pointed the way: in principle, he was a pioneer of the modern environmentalist movement.

Aalto's most attractive and far-reaching efforts to blend industry, housing, and nature into a harmonious whole unfortunately remained unrealized. One of these was his "river rapids center" in Oulu, flanked by the great power plant on one side of the river and by the old town on the other. Another vision that never got off the drawing-board was the linking of large industrial installations along the banks of the river Vuoksi with old villages and new housing areas, forming something that he called a "forest town"—what is today the extremely heterogeneous town of Imatra. Small wonder that after all these abortive efforts Aalto began to despair of "saving the world" with anonymous planning of high quality, and began in the 1950s to concentrate instead on city centers and monumental buildings. This, at least, gave him the opportunity to bestow isolated examples and realized visions on communities who paid little heed to the warnings of nature-lovers and seekers of harmony, while the crisis of industrialism deepened relentlessly.

Aalto started working on the plans for the Sunila Pulp Mill near Kotka with Aulis Kairamo, the engineer responsible for production technology, in autumn 1936. They divided up the manufacturing process between several separate buildings, each having a concrete frame and red brick walls. Warehouses and conveyor installations were built of white concrete. Aalto did only the elevation drawings, and thus had little opportunity to influence the overall design. Much use was made of standardized windows that could be combined to form large, continuous window surfaces. Built of concrete, the lime tower and the warehouse for Glauber's salt contrast with the predominant red brick buildings; the warehouse is an interesting construction of successive concrete arches. In the sulphate warehouse down by the wharf, Aalto found the opportunity to carry out the roof construction with suspended parabolic arches of laminated wood on which he had based his 1934 competition entry for the Helsinki Fair Hall. Even the minor structures—such as a weighing house, a gatehouse, and the fence surrounding the complex—were designed by Aalto. A red brick office building stands on a central "piazza," which forms the heart of the estate. The mill went on line in 1938.

Finnish Pavilion 1937 World's Fair, Paris 1936

THE EXPERIMENTAL, IDEALISTIC, and visionary character that distinguishes many exhibition buildings was eminently suited to Aalto's fundamental architectural persona. His involvement in exhibition planning therefore resulted in a large number of plans and some of his greatest architectural successes. From the early 1930s on, Aalto became increasingly skeptical about the mechanical, antihuman side of Rationalism, and its hostility to nature in particular. This attitude, nourished equally by his love of Finland's nature and folklore and by the Humanist myths about Italy, was the foundation on which he built when creating his most famous exhibition buildings in 1936 and 1938, the Finnish pavilions for the World Fairs of Paris and New York.

Aalto sent in two entries to the 1936 competition for the Finnish Pavilion at the 1937 World's Fair. The result was a triumph for him: the entry "Le bois est en marche" won first prize, and "Tsit Tsit Pum," the bolder of the two entries, placed second.

"Le bois est en marche" formed the basis for the pavilion built by Aalto on the difficult, sloping, wooded site near the Trocadéro that had been allotted to Finland. The ground plan featured an irregular chain of building volumes joined together in a kind of collage. These consisted of small, open, cubic pavilions and two more spacious halls; the hall lower on the slope, a room with a sunken center section with barrel-shaped skylights, was a variant on the principal motif of the Viipuri City Library (page 30). The entire complex curved around a shady garden with Japanese touches, which in the summer heat attracted many visitors for a contemplative stroll. The forest, providing as it does the raw material for Finland's most important industry, was the pavilion's express theme.

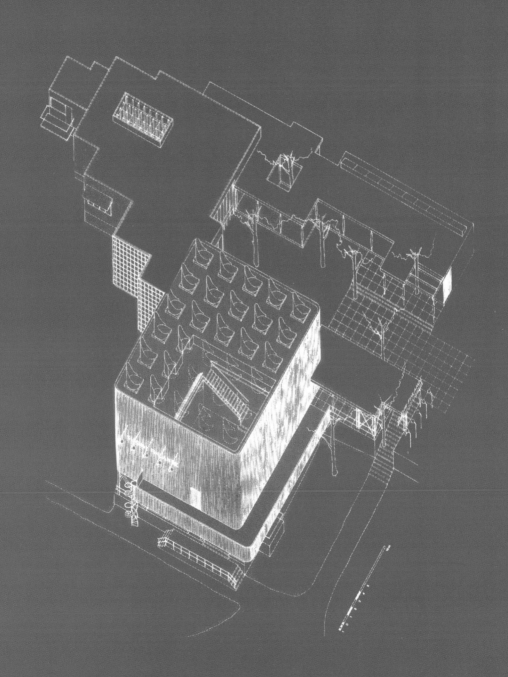

Finnish Pavilion 1939 World's Fair, New York 1938

ALVAR AALTO SUBMITTED two entries ("Maa Kansa Työ Tulos" and "Kas kuusen latvassa oravalla"), and his wife Aino Aalto a third entry ("USA 39") to the 1938 competition. The result was that Alvar won first and second prize and Aino took third. The architects were constrained by the fact that Finland could not afford to build its own pavilion, and had to settle for a small, cubic section of a "unit building" that the host country had allotted to several small nations. The assignment was thus a very limited "furnishing job" that seemed to provide little in the way of either structural interest or facade design. The revelation that prompted Aalto to decide to take part at the last minute was the realization that he could here implement an idea that he had toyed with and given up when designing the Villa Mairea's hall-like living room (page 46). He placed a high, forward-leaning wall with a wavy form suggesting Northern lights along one side of the Finnish "unit" and a free-form balcony on the other. The boxy room was transformed into a tension-filled courtyard, across which the two dramatic facades confronted each other. In the runner-up entry, he conjured away the closed, boxy impression by hanging from the ceiling a kind of gondola containing the cinema called for in the competition program. Aino's entry, also based on sketches for the Villa Mairea hall, consisted of a series of curving, serpentine balconies and a "Venetian" staircase on one side, with a straight balcony on the other. "Maa, Kansa, Työ, Tulos" provided two alternative solutions for the dominating "Northern lights" wall; a third version was finally built. The final drawings, prepared just before and after Aalto's first trip to America, are dated between August 1938 and April 1939.

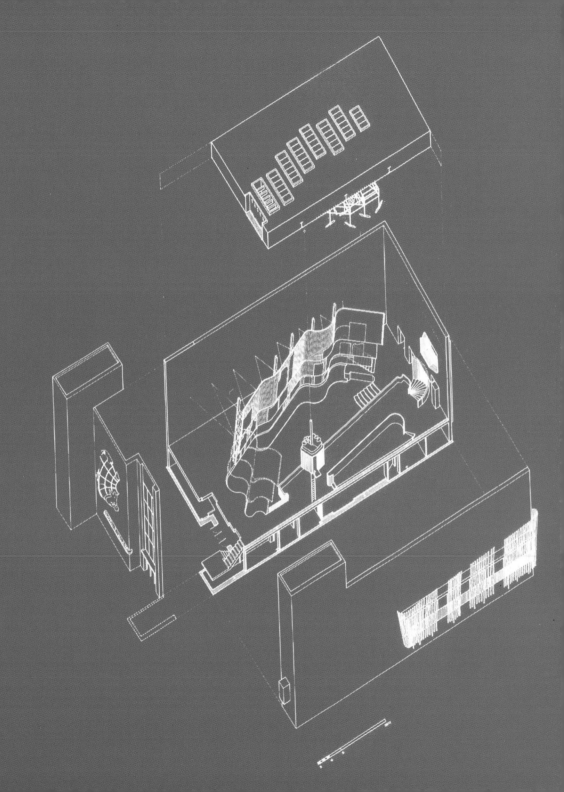

Villa
Mairea

1938

AALTO'S CAREER AS A HOUSING DESIGNER was heralded by a magnificent fanfare: the manor-like house from 1923 for his mother's cousin, surveyor Terho Manner in Töysä. It reflects the vogue for aristocratic country seats that Riitta Nikula has shown to have prevailed in Finland in the 1920s, and which made the Classicist manor the ideal for both farmhouses and summer villas. In Töysä there was even a direct link with the land-owning class that had recently won the Civil War, as the client was the leader of the local defense corps. It is interesting to note that Aalto's split social loyalties revealed themselves even at this early date. Just as he worked simultaneously on designing a building for the defense corps and for workers in Jyväskylä (page 16), so the columned residence in Töysä coincides with the apartment house for railway employees in Jyväskylä and the plan for the Sammallahti industrial area, with its closely studied, health-promoting workers' flats. The fruitful tension between luxury architecture—which gives free rein to artistic inspiration—and a social reform program was even more striking after his "conversion" in 1927 to the modern school of architecture represented by the modern suburbs, the Siedlungen, designed at Bauhaus.

The series of private residences that began in 1932 with the Villa Tammekann in Tartu was modeled on Gropius's masters' housing in Dessau, but Aalto gradually made several softening additions to the matter-of-fact German original, as we see in his own home in Munkkiniemi from 1934 and later in the Sunila site manager's residence. This was partly a matter of using different materials, mainly wood and rendered brick, and a new way of integrating older architectural motifs into the whole, but Aalto's main innovation was a new, non-Euclidean spatial structure closely related to nature's own planning strategy. The crowning achievement, and one of the absolute high-water marks in Aalto's prewar architecture, was the Villa Mairea in Noormarkku. Later events confirmed Aalto's thesis that the results of experiments with new ideas made possible by an exclusive building project can also be used to benefit architecture for ordinary people.

Aalto's relative lack of interest in private houses is evident in the small number of such buildings in his oeuvre, if we exclude the numerous managers' and officials' houses that his extensive assignments for big industrial enterprises called for. A noticeably large proportion of his more individual private houses were designed for personal friends. A significant point was that Aalto combined the owner's professional activities and family life into an indivisible whole. The artist, like any person devoted to his work, cannot draw a clear line between work and leisure. Aalto wished to emphasize the inner coherence of the free, harmonious personality, the fundamental significance of the lifelong vocation. The buildings that he designed for his friends were thus portraits of a kind, images of their unique commitment and personality.

In late winter 1938, Aalto drew up his first plan proposal on 1:100 scale for Maire and Harry Gullichsen's private residence on the Ahlström family estate in Noormarkku, near Pori. The plan comprises an L-shaped building volume with three stories on the entrance side and two facing the walled garden, which contains a sauna and an irregular-shaped swimming pool. An intricate system of mezzanines and stairs leads to a raised inner hall partly encompassing a

free-form studio placed on a higher level. The external wall of the basement level is also in free form, drawn in under the strongly emphasized balcony front of the main floor.

"PROTO-MAIREA." On April 14, 1938, Aalto signed a modified proposal without the raised hall, with the studio rising from the flat third floor. The basement and main story still feature variations of floor height, with various landings and a whole suite of rooms for entertaining guests. A separate art gallery frames the open courtyard beyond the swimming pool. The entrance side has collage-like sections of slate facing, particularly along the projecting balcony of the bedroom story.

VILLA MAIREA AS BUILT. Excavation of the foundation had already begun in spring 1938 to the "Proto-Mairea" plan, when Aalto suddenly decided to delete the entire basement, combining the drawing rooms and the initially separate art gallery into a large "all-purpose room." This resulted in two clear-cut, comprehensive floor plans, with the ground floor reserved for entertaining and the top floor strictly for private life. The porte-cochère has a colonnade of unstripped saplings supporting a free-form roof. A few steps lead up from the entrance hall to the living room, which combines the multipurpose character of a peasant cottage (suggested by the monumental open fireplace) with a "forest space" disposition inspired by modern painting (particularly the work of Cézanne). Aalto had previously experimented with such spaces, open to the surrounding nature,

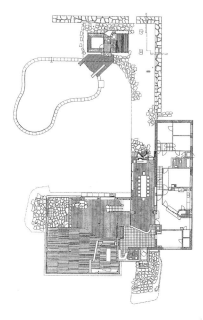

SAUNA, DETAIL

MAIN STAIRCASE, LIVING ROOM

LIVING ROOM, VIEW TOWARD
MAIN ENTRANCE

in his plan for the Finnish pavilion at the 1937 World's Fair in Paris (page 42). From this room, like a concentrated forest image, a staircase bordered by irregularly composed wooden poles leads up to the upper floor, which contains a painting studio, bedrooms, children's rooms, and playroom as well as a number of guestrooms. The courtyard is framed by the L-shaped villa, with the dining room and kitchen area at the lowest level, and the transversely placed sauna and irregular swimming pool along the third side. The painting studio rises up like a tower from the upper floor level, clad with wooden poles stained brown; the remaining facades have irregular, white-rendered brick surfaces. Fixed and movable furnishings are exquisite in every detail, the main materials being wood, stone, and ceramic tile. The villa is undisputably the crowning achievement of the young Aalto's architectural oeuvre. The last of the 422 final working drawings is dated January 1, 1939.

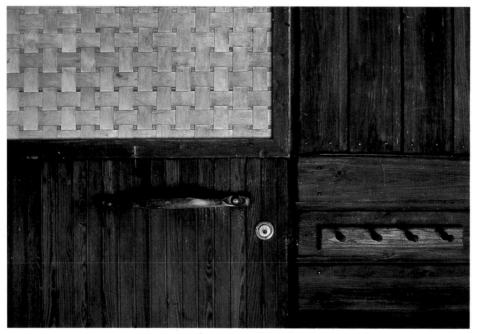

Baker House, MIT

1946

THE MASSACHUSETTS INSTITUTE of Technology, near Boston, where Aalto had been appointed research fellow in 1940, commissioned him in 1946 to design a student dormitory next to the busy shoreline drive along the Charles River. Aalto considered it psychologically inappropriate to have the rooms with a view directly face the incessant flow of cars; at the same time, he wished to have as many rooms as possible face the sun and the river. The solution was to give the house a meandering serpentine form, increasing the length of the facade and producing oblique views. Moreover, each room took on an individual form, in line with Aalto's wish to counteract technocratic uniformity. The north side is occupied mostly by secondary spaces, such as the common rooms, corridors, and an original stair system that expands upward in fanlike consoles from the control desk in the ground-floor entrance hall. The financial calculations were based on cost per bed, which forced Aalto to maximize the number of rooms. In order to avoid dark corridors, he placed the student canteen and cafeteria in a low, separate wing facing the river in front of the serpentine facade, and added several rooms in a fan arrangement at the west end. He was asked in late 1947 to complete the working drawings for the dormitory together with the local architects' office of Parrey, Shaw & Hepburn; construction began soon after. The main wing is seven stories high, the six upper floors being occupied exclusively by students' rooms. The main facade material is unevenly fired brick, though grey marble was used for the low, square restaurant wing. The restaurant is lit by round barrel skylights in the flat roof, above which a system of suspended electric lights provide lighting in the dark hours of the day. Aalto wished to cover the south facade of the main wing with ivy clinging to a trellis, and to have a large rooftop garden,

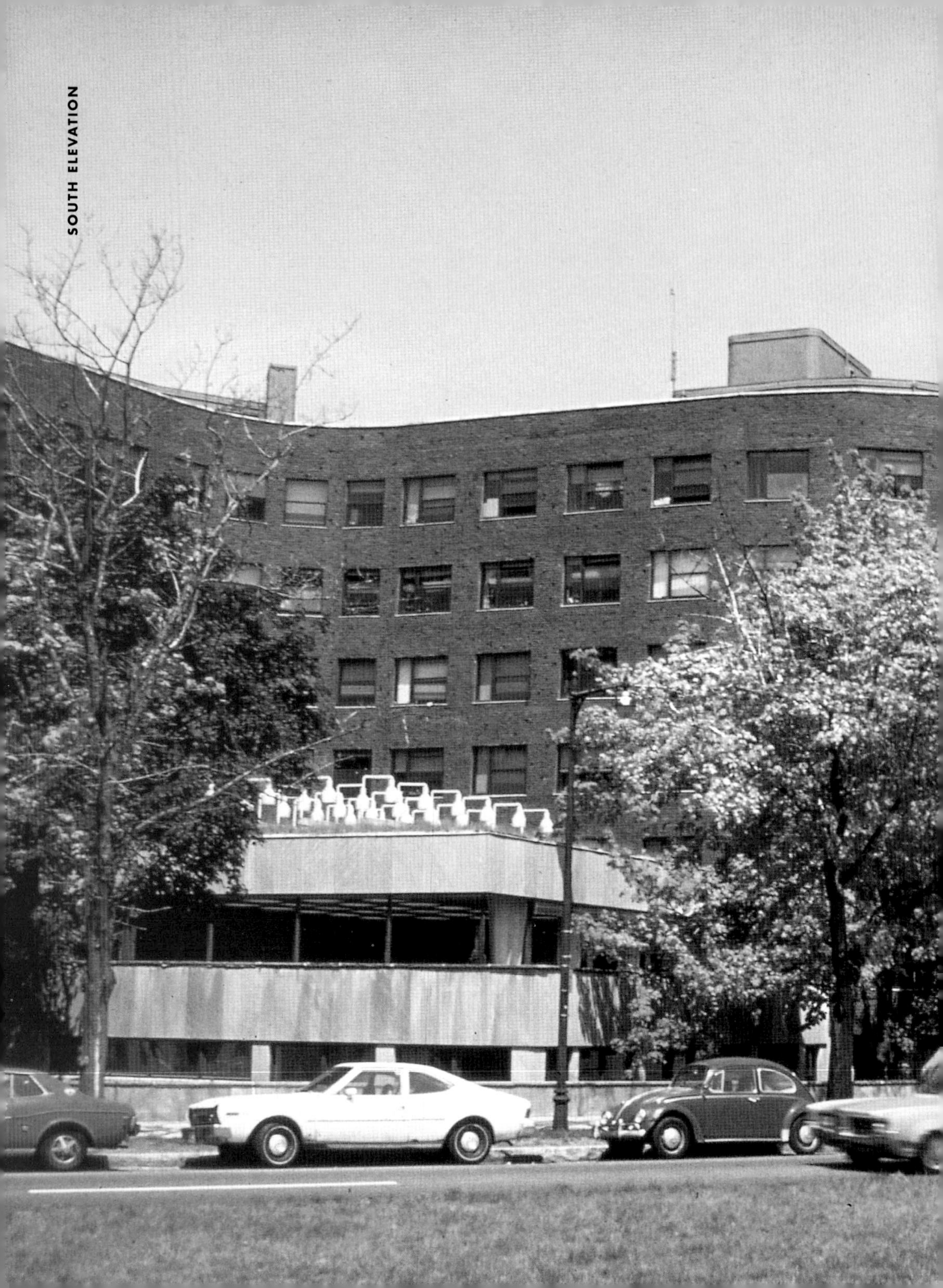

SOUTH ELEVATION

but these plans were scrapped for financial reasons. The high-quality furnishings of the student rooms were designed by Aino Aalto, and the furniture was delivered in January 1949 by Svenska Artek, whereas the fixtures were made by the American manufacturer Cory. The dormitory was inaugurated in June 1949.

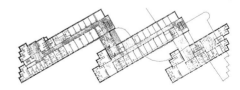

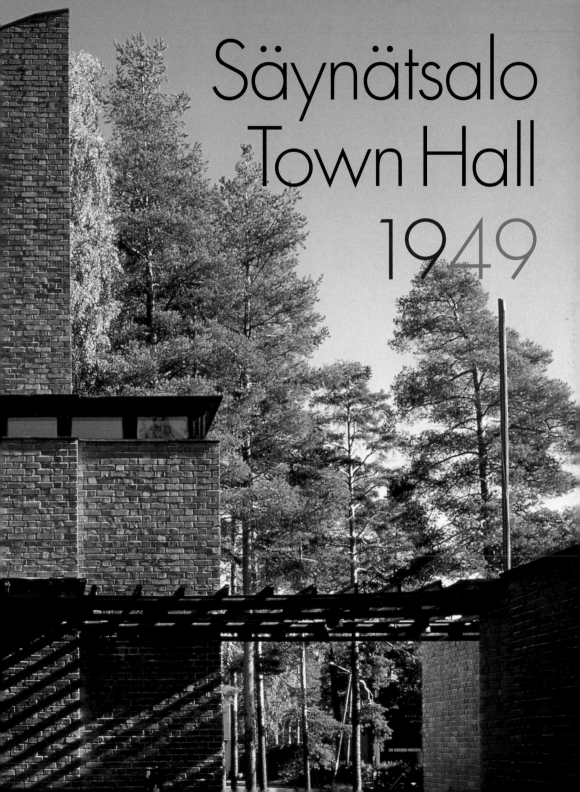

Säynätsalo
Town Hall
1949

AALTO HAD A SPONTANEOUSLY anarchistic personality: anti-authoritarian, unwilling to accept restraints or standardizing rules. He believed that society could be based on the principle of free will, a sense of community, the open meeting of free, congenial minds. One might think that the task he set himself in 1923, designing a parliament building for newly independent Finland, was wholly alien to his nature. In fact his plan was something of an unconscious provocation, a calling into question of the conventions of parliamentary work. Giving a modicum of attention to the room generally considered the most important—the legislative chamber—he instead produced two oversized subsidiary spaces: the library and the restaurant. He placed the library in a gigantic separate wing, where members could freely consult the opinions of independent authors and commune with the great minds of world literature. As for the magnificent restaurant, it was to lure members of Parliament into informal debates with the public at common meals, providing a setting for inspiring symposia.

Interestingly, Aalto took a completely different view of the governing bodies of cities and municipalities. He probably felt that small-scale local government provides an effective forum for the direct, individual, voluntary assumption of responsibility he wished to build upon. Somewhere in the background looms the administrative model of the city-states of ancient Greece and the Italian Renaissance, which Aalto greatly idealized. As early as the 1920s, he dreamed of making Jyväskylä a provincial capital with a sumptuous monumental building for the provincial government, and in the 1960s he still wished to create, in his plan for the House of Finnish Architecture, an arena where the country's cities would compete—like Siena, Florence, and Venice of yore—with prestigious architectural masterworks.

Aalto's aim was to restore to monumentality an absolute value as a manifestation of the prestige needs of cities; this contrasted sharply with the anonymous matter-of-factness of Functionalism and provided an expression for his opposition to Rationalism. The Avesta Town Hall plan in 1944 and the Säynätsalo Town Hall plan five years later reveal the stratagems to which Aalto resorted in order to confer upon the seats of local government the monumentality possessed by the town halls of old, even though the council chamber and reception rooms no longer take up the bulk of the town hall's space. To make these buildings sufficiently impressive, he included in both a series of secondary functions foreign to local government. In Avesta these included a hotel, a "House of the People," a library, and a theater; in Säynätsalo, a library, shops, and flats.

Another problem was that fiscal administration requires considerably more space than the chamber where the decisions are made, with the result that many town halls look more like ordinary office buildings than symbols of power. Aalto's solution was to emphasize the relatively small council chamber by placing it in a conspicuously separate location or giving it an interesting form that makes it stand out psychologically as the most important section of the complex. An extreme example is his plan for the German city of Castrop-Rauxel, but the idea is the same in the town hall plans for Gothenburg, Rovaniemi, and Jyväskylä.

Aalto's town halls have another psychological focus besides the council chamber: he usually gave a prominent position to a "Citizens' Square." We find one in the Avesta plan and

at Säynätsalo; it reappears in Seinäjoki (page 150), Rovaniemi, and government centers.

It should be strongly emphasized that the striving for prestigious monumentality that distinguishes a few of Aalto's government buildings—though, in line with his philosophy, this is more characteristic of his plans for cultural buildings—was of a highly idiosyncratic nature. Riitta Nikula, head of research at the Museum of Finnish Architecture, has pointed out the distinctive characteristics of the various entries to the 1924 competition for the Finnish Parliament House. All of them used Classicist forms, but whereas J. S. Sirén's winning and later realized plan was the most monumental in its blocklike massiveness, Aalto's was the most obviously Italianate. Aalto had not yet visited Italy at the time, but his teachers at the Institute of Technology had instilled in him a lively interest in the Italian urban environment, and from Gunnar Asplund he had learned the playful Classicism liberated from orthodox period style that Ragnar Östberg had introduced before Asplund. Aalto's Parliament House entry was monumental in the same way that the Italian townscape is: polyphonic, adapted to the terrain, human in scale.

Aalto's conversion to Functionalism did not bring any change in this point, as his intricate 1944 plan for the Avesta town hall shows. The argument for fragmenting the massive building volume into smaller but coordinated parts, however, was here more closely related to function than before. Blocklike conglomerate buildings such as the Defense Corps Building in Jyväskylä and the Agricultural Cooperative Building in Turku no longer appear: they are replaced by multifaceted building complexes that look like whole city districts even though they serve a centralized activity. Aalto's attitude to monumentality was particularly evident in his efforts to "save" Sirén's Parliament House from an excessively authoritarian emphasis by integrating it in his plan for the new center of Helsinki. A component in a polyphonic but concordant cityscape, it was to be provided with rivals in the form of various cultural buildings, in the same way as the Palace of the Doges in Venice is only one of the components of one of the world's most admired architectural settings.

For Säynätsalo Aalto had drawn up a master plan for the industrial community in 1942–47, indicating a site for the future municipal offices. The local authorities inquired as early as 1947 whether he would design the building, and he probably drew the first sketches at this time, but consideration for the two other colleagues approached, Seppo Hytönen and Veikko Raitinen, prompted him to recommend a competition to which all three architects were invited and for which they were guaranteed an equal fee of 80,000 marks. Aalto won the competition in January 1949 with an entry marked "Curia," and was immediately commissioned to prepare working drawings. Completed in 1952, the building is one of Aalto's most admired designs. It marks the end of his years in the United States, and can be taken as a paean to everything he felt to be crucial about the European tradition: small-scale democracy, individualism, harmony with nature, civilized moderation, disdain of ostentation, and superficial effects.

The building has a variety of functions. Seat of the municipal council and administration, it also contains the local lending library; rented space for a bank, a pharmacy, a barber's shop; and more; and housing for municipal employees. Aalto laid out four two-story wings

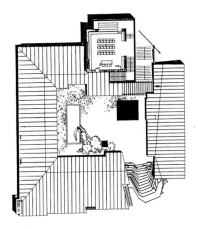

around a square courtyard set one story higher than its surroundings. The courtyard is entered by a terraced, grassy slope at the open west corner and by a staircase to the east corner. Apartments occupy one of the wings; the businesses face outward from the ground floors of the remaining three wings; and the administrative and cultural facilities look inward to the quiet courtyard. From the beginning, the idea was that the municipal offices could expand into the housing and business facilities. This has in fact happened over the years: thus, the library has taken over the shop that was originally beneath it. The main material used for the exterior as well as for the representative areas of the interior is bare red brick. The dominant element of the building is the council chamber, which soars towerlike above the complex. This monumental, elegantly simple room is enlivened by spare side-lighting filtered through wooden louvers and by two technically innovative roof trusses justified by the need for ventilation between the ceiling and roof. The entire interior, including fixtures, furnishings, and lighting, was designed specially by Aalto.

In describing his plan for the municipal offices, which Aalto preferred to call a "town hall," he wrote: "I used the enclosed courtyard as the principal motif because in some mysterious way it emphasizes the social instinct. In government buildings and town halls, the courtyard has preserved its primal significance from the days of ancient Crete, Greece, and Rome through the Middle Ages and the Renaissance. Buildings with central courtyards also have the shortest corridors in relation to room area. Central corridors or dark passageways cannot and should not be used in administrative buildings."

Hakasalmi Oy Commercial Building ("Rautatalo") 1951

AALTO'S BUSINESS OFFICES differ in one crucial point from his government buildings. He never idealized economic power as such, and was no promoter of the capitalist system, though he did receive many major commissions from big industry. None of his bank offices or company headquarters assert the client's power in the way that most American skyscrapers do. One should perhaps make an exception here for the provocative marble palace that houses the Enso-Gutzeit headquarters in Helsinki. For Aalto, however, this was not a matter of glorifying the state-owned wood-processing company, but of adding an appropriate element to the city's appearance on a prominent site.

Nevertheless, Aalto strove to give the central buildings that he designed for the business world a more striking appearance than that of an ordinary apartment or office block. He even once wrote a newspaper article in which he inveighed against "the American Main Street town, Mr. Babbitt's petty bourgeois ideal of building complexes," characterized by "an amorphous blend of public and commercial buildings with housing." He considered the placing of public buildings "as important as that of the vital organs in the human body," and felt that business buildings should provide decorous accents in the urban landscape.

The most important thing for Aalto, however, was to make these buildings pleasant places to work, as his showpiece, the National Pensions Institute in Helsinki (page 96), demonstrates with particular clarity. The entire plan was aimed at providing the staff with a milieu that would be as practically laid out, as close to nature, and as free of an oppressive anthill atmosphere as possible. But Aalto did not shy away from providing the management with a little extra quality of life compared to the rank and file. For him, particularly lavish furnishings were justified as pointers for the future and as cultural attainments that he hoped would later benefit a greater number of people. The extraordinary rise in the general standard of living (and, naturally, the attendant problems that arose) during Aalto's lifetime encouraged him to continue on his course of constantly seeking to make better and more comfortable buildings—first for the privileged few who could afford his experiments, and then on a larger scale for the many.

Aalto's business buildings show obvious affinities with international models. His first major bank plan, the 1926 competition entry for the Union Bank in Helsinki, was based—like the winning entry by P. E. Blomstedt that was built—on a type of American commercial building that preceded the skyscraper proper. The Guaranty Building by D. Adler and Louis Sullivan might be named as an obvious example. From 1927, Le Corbusier's strip windows and smooth wall surfaces dominated Aalto's idiom, but as early as 1937 and 1943, Aalto sought a more monumental look for this type of building in his offices at Sunila and Varkaus, clad in red brick and characterized

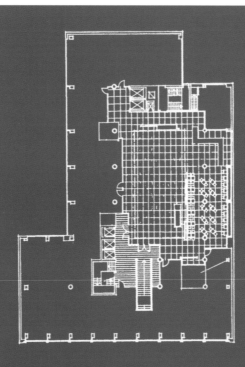

by massive cubism. This trend culminated in the "Forum Redivivum" entry in the National Pensions Institute competition, and in a handful of cultural buildings from the same period.

Once the war reparations to the Soviet Union had been paid off in the early 1950s, Finland eagerly set out to establish links with the expanding economy of the West, and luxurious business complexes such as Rautatalo from 1951 and Viljo Revell's Teollisuuskeskus of 1952 pioneered a new Finnish commercial architecture. Aalto later provided a large number of both cultural and commercial buildings with modular facades of square windows framed by white marble or sheet metal. He avoided monotony by stepping the facades, as in the east side of the Enso-Gutzeit palazzo, or by the free placing of buildings in an urban milieu. His later office plans, such as that for the BP building in Hamburg, break down the massive building volume into towerlike components. The idea was to provide the various offices with both seclusion and internal communication by means of a characteristic "invention": a meandering arrangement of rooms with contiguous corners. His goal was a vital, lifelong preoccupation: to save the "little man" from collectivization and mechanization.

For this building, in the heart of Helsinki, Aalto sent in the entry "Casa" to the 1951 invitational competition. The client was the Finnish hardware dealers' federation, whence the building's name (which means "iron house" in English). Aalto's plan won first prize and was used as the basis for implementation in 1952–57. From the start, his main theme was a large interior light court behind an austere, copper-clad facade, which he sought to harmonize with the neighboring building designed by Eliel Saarinen in 1920. Aalto, however, gradually had to pare away at his original vision of a Nordic counterpart to the "Galleries" in Milan. In the competition version, the covered courtyard with barrel skylights extended from first floor to the seventh, top story, with five travertine-faced gallery levels suspended between them. The client, however, complained about lost office space. Aalto stubbornly held out for three gallery levels, but finally had to settle for two. With its Aalto-designed café for 120 people, its purling little fountain, and the surrounding exclusive boutiques (including Aalto's own furniture company, Artek), this light court was one of the city's most pleasant oases until debased by a vulgar Americanization in the mid-1980s. In the building's regular squared facade of copper and glass, the display window axes of the two bottom floors correspond to the office window axes of the two top floors. The building is separated from its neighbors by visible red-brick fire walls. The light court is reached from the street level by a Venetian staircase with walls clad with ceramic tiles of various colors. Apart from the two lower stories, occupied by shops, the building consists entirely of small but high-quality offices. Aalto first designed the organically formed bronze door handle which is a hallmark of his later buildings for the Rautatalo.

Seinäjoki Church

1951–56

AS NOTED IN THE FIRST volume of my Aalto biography, *The Early Years*, it was something of a paradox that Aalto, to whom religious dogma was totally alien and who had an almost Voltairean antipathy to the Church, devoted so much time and effort to designing churches and other religious architecture (pp. 188ff.). In the same context, however, an attempt was made to establish that there was, after all, a tenable ideological reason for Aalto's involvement with sacred buildings. Not that he was moved by the mystique of suffering preached by Christian doctrine any more than by its transcendental ideas of the hereafter; instead, he had a deeply held belief in the inherent harmony of existence that the Greek philosophers called *kosmos*. This involves a constantly renewed equilibrium in nature and in human life, in which everything must be in correct proportion to the totality of things.

The idea lends itself to formal expression, to harmonious architectural forms and carefully weighed juxtapositions of manmade and natural forms. For Aalto, however, this had nothing to do with formalist games or aesthetic coquetry, but with the central problem of life. This element gives all of Aalto's architecture an air of sacredness, just as all objects—even the simplest utensils of everyday life—in ancient Egypt, in China, or on the South Sea Islands have a connection with religion. What distinguishes Aalto's churches from his other architecture is the effort he made to define in them his creed of a supreme, timeless, pure, universal order.

Aalto's earliest church designs show a strong Italian influence. This connection remained throughout his life, but it was tempered in the 1930s by the Functionalist idiom and later increasingly by the organic thinking that governed his mature architecture.

An ingredient in much of Aalto's architecture that is particularly prominent in some of his church designs is their financially motivated multiple use. For much of his life, Aalto had to adapt to straitened economic conditions, first during the depression between the wars and then during postwar reconstruction. Efforts in the 1920s and '30s to provide better housing for the masses were geared to the modern minimum apartment, for which Aalto's 1929 sofabed is a fitting symbol. Designing churches in the postwar years, he readily thought of them as sofabeds of a kind: usable equally as large, monumental churches and as practical everyday facilities, and also, if possible, as stages for gigantic open-air festivities. In today's affluent society, Aalto's sliding inner walls and flexible auditoria are used ever less, as they require extra work, and alternative localities are available. Whether this means a lasting change in the demands made on architecture remains to be seen.

Another aspect of Aalto's churches is that in terms of form they are more traditional than his other works. Campaniles, basilica forms, and lingering symmetry recur right to the very end of his career. The reason must be that when faced with the ultimate questions and the ceremonies of birth and death, we tend to cling to past customs more than in everyday life. Nevertheless, here as in other fields, Aalto succeeded in renewing tradition and opening up new perspectives for the people of a new age.

Aalto took part in a competition for a large church and parish center announced by Seinäjoki parish in 1951, sending in an entry marked "Lakeuden risti" (Cross of the Plains).

Instead of placing the parish rooms under the church or in a smaller, separate building, as the other entrants had done, Aalto seized upon the big religious events commonly organized in Ostrobothnia in summer. He laid out a large piazza, sloping down toward the church and girded by the parish facilities, in front of the church's main facade. This space-consuming solution obliged Aalto to exceed the prescribed construction limit by some twenty meters, which prevented the jury from awarding him a prize. The prize sum was therefore divided equally between three less striking entries (submitted by architecture students), but the jury awarded Aalto's entry a purchase and recommended it as the basis for implementation. Aalto's design also included, south of the church, a vicarage with apartments for the vicar and two chaplains.

In 1956 Aalto was commissioned to develop the plan further. The church was built between 1958 and 1960 and the large parish center in front between 1964 and 1966.

The church was basically built to the competition design, except that Aalto had hoped to use black granite as the facade material; for reasons of cost, however, he had to be content with brick rendered white, with only the side chapel being faced with granite. The main characteristics of the church complex are as follows: on the north side stands the campanile, 65 meters high, in the shape of a stylized cross. Monumentally vertical, visible from afar in the endless plains, it is the town's symbol. The slightly wedge-shaped, symmetrical church interior is 47 meters long and provides seating for a congregation of 1,400. Despite the rudimentary aisles outside the bearing columns, the church speaks the language of modernism with the constructivist form of its columns, the freely formed wing of the pulpit, the cubist organ facade, the expressionist design of the chandeliers, and the merging of vertical and horizontal in the window system. Seen from outside in the winter darkness, the church looks like a row of gigantic burning candles standing in the snow. The vestry lies behind the altar, and between it and the campanile is a tiny baptistry and wedding chapel with a stained-glass work by Aalto. Aalto also designed the church textiles and communion vessels. The parish center's main divergence from the competition entry is the open staircase on an axis from the main facade of the church to the town hall square (built up later). This staircase separates the two wings of the building, which contain a large assembly hall, catering facilities for the congregation, a room for confirmation classes, a clubroom, offices, and several apartments for employees. Both wings are from one to two stories high, in brick rendered white. Besides the three apartments for the vicar and two chaplains, the vicarage plan included a heating plant for the entire complex. Only the heating plant and, later, two apartments for service staff were built.

In a description of the center of Seinäjoki dated May 9, 1969 (in the Aalto archives), Aalto wrote: "The whole center began with—the church. Around it developed the cluster of other public buildings, which never would have been possible without the church's initiative. The church, which in view of its size could be called a cathedral, has provided the yardstick of scale and quality in the origin and present form of the center of Seinäjoki."

NATIONAL PENSIONS INSTITUTE, 1952

National
Pensions Institute

1952

IN 1948 AINO AND ALVAR AALTO won a competition to design an office complex in Helsinki for the National Pensions Institute. The entire original plan was scrapped in 1952, however, when a much smaller, triangular site in Taka-Töölö (bordered by Nordenskiöldinkatu, Messeniuksenkatu, and Minna Canthinkatu) was selected. None of the commercial and cultural buildings included in the initial plan could be fitted in, only the offices. In order to avoid the oppressive feeling of a large office building in a crowded urban setting, Aalto differentiated the workplaces for over 800 employees into an organism spread out among several seemingly individual building volumes with excellent internal communications both above and below ground. The complex forms an irregular U surrounding a raised, planted courtyard sheltered from traffic noise and exhaust gases and with a view of an adjacent park; the height of the building volumes is stepped down toward the park. The general public has access only to the customer service hall, three stories high and lit by three prism-shaped lantern skylights. This room originally contained twenty-eight unroofed interview cubicles in which applicants could present their cases undisturbed to the staff; the cubicles were removed, however, when the local office for Helsinki pensioners moved out. Of special interest is the tiny library, which contains specialist insurance literature and books lent out to the staff; it is a miniature version of Aalto's renowned early work, the Viipuri Library (page 30), which Finland lost to Russia in the war.

LIBRARY

The facade materials are red brick, copper, and black granite. The building is distinguished throughout by workmanship and materials of high quality: all details are carefully studied and the interior design is exquisite, especially that of the management floor and the conference rooms. Aalto developed several new variants of his standard furniture for the Institute, a whole series of new light fittings, ceramic wall claddings, and a variety of textiles. Work on the plans went on from 1953 to 1957; construction began in March 1954 and was completed two and a half years later. The complex comprises 310 rooms and 22,500 square meters of floor space.

Describing the building, Aalto noted: "Although the building is equipped with mechanical ventilation connected with the heating system, the architect wished to provide every room with the biological advantages of natural airing and a window that can be opened" (*Arkkitehti*, no. 1–2, 1958).

House of Culture

1955

THE FINNISH COMMUNIST PARTY, through its representative Matti Janhunen, asked Aalto in 1952 to draw up plans for a building complex combining the party headquarters, association facilities, and a cultural center on a recently acquired site beneath the Alppiharju cliffs in Helsinki. The sketches did not take definitive form until 1955, when construction finally got under way. The house was inaugurated in 1958. Aalto tackled the job as three separate assignments, giving the building a tripartite structure. Originally the whole complex was to be faced with red brick, but the plans later changed. Aalto built a rectangular, copper-clad office wing with five stories above ground and a large, free-form auditorium of red brick connected by a lower wing, forming a small piazza. The office wing contains 110 offices, meeting and conference rooms, and hobby rooms. The connecting wing contains a lobby and cloakroom, a lecture auditorium, three classrooms, five meeting rooms, a library, and a large gymnasium at basement level. The main rooms of the auditorium wing are a large congress and concert hall with seating for 1,500, a restaurant, and a small basement cinema (today used as a meeting room). The whole complex is held together by a column-borne copper canopy that runs alongside the street for 60 meters and forms a portico to the little piazza, which features a fountain by Wäinö Aaltonen in the form of an open hand.

The basic idea of contrasting free-form red brick walls with a cubic mass originated in the MIT dormitory plan (page 66), in which the restaurant wing fulfills a similar function in front

of the brick facade. The main point of interest in the House of Culture is the asymmetrical auditorium, in which Aalto perfected the idea of the backward-growing rear wall introduced in the Kuopio Theater entry and later adapted for the Essen Opera House (page 170) and Finlandia Hall (page 198) designs. According to Aalto, the form of the House of Culture auditorium was dictated by acoustic considerations: "The various uses of the room require first-class acoustics, which is the reason for the form, a concrete helix combined with wood and brick. Specially designed wall and ceiling surfaces both absorb and reflect sound waves. Substitute wall panels can be used for various acoustic needs—for an empty or full house, for concerts or congresses—without disrupting the architectural rhythm" (vol. 1 in the Artemis edition, p. 188). Aalto's hopes were fulfilled: the House of Culture became known for its excellent acoustics, and is used frequently for concerts as well as orchestra rehearsals and recordings. The monolithic exterior of the auditorium wing, which closely follows the helical form of the interior and is almost windowless, displays variously bent brick surfaces, which could not have been built without the specially manufactured standard wedge-shaped brick invented by Aalto for the purpose.

Declared a historic national monument in 1989, the building was meticulously restored in 1990–91 and sold by the Communist Party to a nonprofit organization shortly thereafter.

MAIN AUDITORIUM

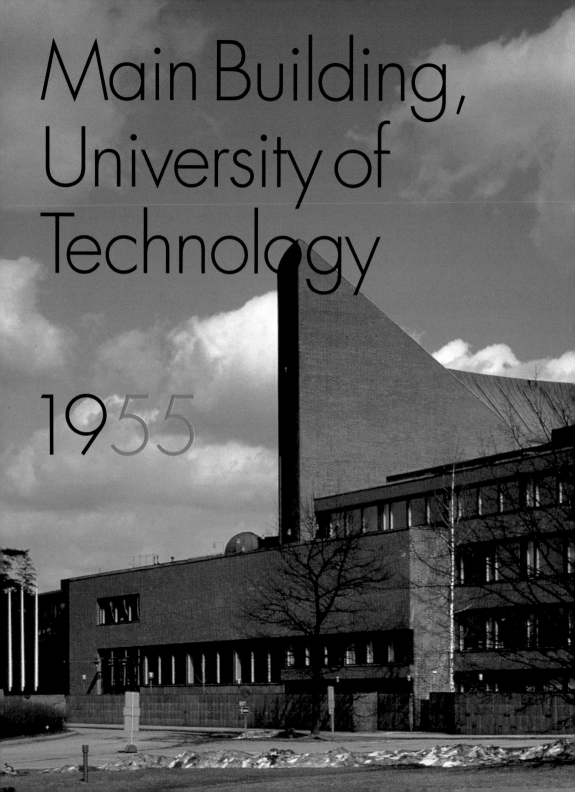

Main Building, University of Technology

1955

AALTO'S CONTRIBUTIONS in the sector of "cultural buildings" are most easily considered by means of the gateway for most people to the world of systematic culture: school. Aalto's kindergartens were as a rule built in industrial communities by the major industrial enterprises that dominated them. It should be noted that Aino Aalto, who was mainly responsible for these projects, was a firm adherent of Maria Montessori's ideas on promoting children's spontaneous activity and free upbringing.

The buildings designed by Aalto for later stages of education were no reformatories, either: in his philosophy, they were clearly linked with the principle of individual free will. In a speech he delivered at the centenary of his own school, Jyväskylä Lyceum, he said that the most important lesson he learned there was what he called the gift of doubt, the ability to form a critical, independent opinion about doctrines and value judgments.

Compulsory school education was introduced in Finland in 1921, leading to a boom in school construction. In the 1920s and '30s an average of 150 school buildings were erected every year. Many were built to established type plans, but occasionally local building traditions were followed. This was the case with the first schoolhouse designed by Aalto, the dual elementary school of Kauhajärvi and Lappajärvi. His second major primary education assignment, Inkeroinen elementary school, was built just before the deadline established by legislation on the construction of elementary schools. This design was pronouncedly Functionalist, and its nearest parallel is seen in Gunnar Taucher's similar school buildings in Helsinki. Aalto's last school design was the teacher training school for the Jyväskylä University campus. The division into small, vertically grouped sections, intended to break the monotony of the long school building's large scale, was unique for the period and constituted an important psychological innovation.

Aalto took it for granted that those privileged people who had the opportunity to study at universities and colleges should be animated equally by critical independence and intellectual curiosity. He had a considerable respect for academic titles, and liked to make friends with learned professors and specialists of the humanities. His academic ambitions went so far that he called his architectural office in Munkkiniemi "my academy," since he instructed his younger assistants there. This attitude made it easy for him to lend all the dignity an institution of higher learning could desire to the many universities he designed. His first effort in the field was a competition entry in 1931 for an annex to the University of Helsinki. Aalto's plan, closely related to P. E. Blomstedt's entry, represented Functionalism, in contrast to J. S. Sirén's Classicist design that was carried out between 1933 and 1937. The competitions for the Helsinki University of Technology at Otaniemi and the Institute of Pedagogics in Jyväskylä reactivated Aalto's interest in buildings for higher education. His plans introduced to Finland the Anglo-Saxon principle of grouping the university buildings together around a campus, a solution with which his work as a professor at MIT near Boston had made him familiar. The University of Technology campus consists of a dominating main building in a parklike setting, ringed by the library and laboratory buildings. Most of Aalto's university plans include laboratories, which are particularly prominent in the 1944 plans for the Johnson Institute in Avesta, which combine functionality with high architectural quality.

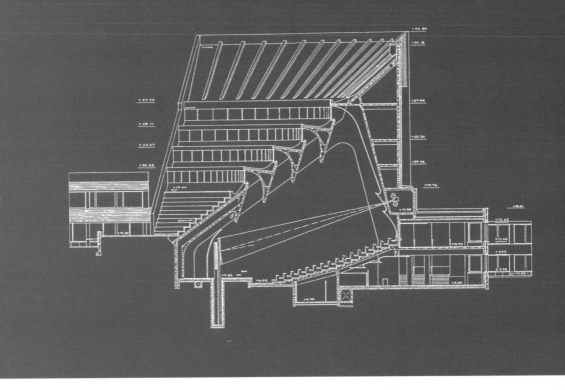

After Aalto had won the competition for the University of Technology's new placing in Otaniemi outside the Helsinki city limits in 1949, a long-drawn-out period of development began in 1953, the basic design of the main building being completed in 1955. Construction did not begin until 1964, but the building was inaugurated September 1, 1966, though furnishing work continued until 1967. The building is one of Aalto's most powerful statements, and in its unaffected simplicity one of his most convincing designs. Its centerpoint is the towerlike, bevelled cylinder segment that soars from the high point of the site, where the Otaniemi manor house once stood in a park now integrated into the university campus. This motif is a development of the auditorium design—reminiscent of the Classical theater cavea—introduced by Aalto in the Zagreb Central Hospital entry. The original building program included an assembly hall seating an audience of 1,000, but its construction was postponed for financial reasons. Aalto wanted to keep in store the possibility of building this auditorium maximum by placing in the tower two auditoria with identical cross sections, one seating 576 listeners and the other 327, separated by a temporary partition. Basically these form a single cavea, with staggered tiers in the shape of a circle segment rhythmically echoed by the steep rise of the roof, in which vertical "stair" surfaces are replaced by rows of windows. The two large, adjacent auditoria, furnished with acoustic wall elements, project a magnificent sense of space.

Around this centerpiece, which has an entrance hall at ground level, the other parts of the building complex (considerably lower) are grouped irregularly on stories 1–4 like dominoes

that can be linked as needed, forming smaller courtyard patterns. On the third floor to one side of the tower is the administrative section with the principal's office, council room, etc.; on the second floor is a rectangular auditorium and hall space; and on the ground floor the teachers' and students' cafeterias. On the other side are classrooms for first- and second-year general studies, a physics laboratory lit by oblong prisms in the roof, an auditorium for 310 listeners, and the departments of surveying and architecture. One cannot help suspecting that Aalto favored these two departments that were closest to his heart; the other departments, with their laboratories, classrooms, etc., are in separate buildings designed by other architects.

In exterior planning, Aalto—true to his principles—separated motorized traffic on the outside of the complex from pedestrian traffic on the inside, where green lawns and pathways to the other departments and student housing form a peaceful campus. At the lower tip of the tower, Aalto built a small open-air theater as a termination to the staggered roof, a place for students to gather informally for discussions, sunbathing, or even to listen to the principal's speeches from an adjacent window in the administrative wing. The main materials used for the building are black granite, specially manufactured dark red brick, and copper. All of the departments are designed so as to accommodate enlargement without damaging the overall impression.

The first enlargement of the main building took place between 1966 and 1976, consisting of a new two-story office wing on the south side and new auditoria and other additional space on the west.

In a description dated February 2, 1955, and attached by Aalto to the plans for the main building, he wrote: "For financial reasons, we have tried to make do without decorative additions; that is, the intention was to produce an architectural form that in itself lends the building the academic dignity due to the main building of a large university, without resorting to decorative techniques."

In *Arkkitehti*, he explained the use of marble for the architecture department, which aroused strong opposition among spartan students toward the end of this "revolutionary" decade: "Marble has been used for the places which are eventually intended to house a collection of architectural fragments, as especially the collection's historical parts will harmonize best with this material. This collection, which will certainly take time to develop, corresponds in the teaching of architecture to the other departments' laboratories, and must therefore be placed on a par with them in budgeting" (no. 4, 1966). For his fragment collection, Aalto hoped to acquire objects such as Classical columns from Italy. So far the whole idea has been ignored.

Church of the Three Crosses

1955–58

AALTO'S CHURCH PLANS from the 1920s differ fairly sharply from the designs typical for the times. None of them were conventional hall churches with end towers. His strongly Italianate plans from this period include those for the churches of Taulumäki and Muurame, hall churches with a freestanding campanile. The forms are ascetic, with sparing ornamentation alluding to various eras. In other words, these church plans can be called historicist.

The competitions for the churches of Taulumäki and Töölö fall stylistically in the transition from Classicism to Functionalism. To the competitions for the churches of Vallila, Tehtaanpuisto, and Temppeliaukio, Aalto sent boldly Functionalist plans that were not appreciated by the Classically inclined juries. Then followed a long period during which he did not take part in competitions for religious buildings, nor did he receive any commissions from parishes.

Seventeen years passed before he participated in the competitions for Lahti Church and the Malmi funeral chapel, winning first prize in both, his breakthrough as a church architect. His church designs from the 1950s and '60s tend toward the sculpturesque, a tendency that culminated in this project, known as the Vuoksenniska Church. The wedge, or fan plan, which appeared as early as 1929 in the competition entry for Vallila Church, returned in more or less pronounced form in almost all of Aalto's postwar churches. He achieved individuality and intimacy by endowing his church interiors with free form, and by treating the various parts of the building in a highly unconventional manner. In Vuoksenniska and Riola the ceiling developed into a key motif that dominated and powerfully molded the whole interior. One is tempted to say that

Aalto's churches from the 1950s and '60s are unique sculptural monuments, an architecture for which there is no parallel.

Aalto started working on the plans for this church at Vuoksenniska in 1955 as an off-shoot of the master plan of Imatra completed in 1953. Construction of the church was completed in 1958. Without any doubt Aalto's most original church design, Vuoksenniska Church—in conformity with his fundamental approach to architecture as a synthesis of varied practical and aesthetic needs—fuses a broad range of motifs into a unique, coherent work of artistic perfection.

I cannot resist the temptation of quoting Aalto's own description of the conscious elements on which he built—the unconscious ones were dictated by his mature experience. He started by citing a problem that he had solved in a completely different way in Seinäjoki Church (page 90), the conflict between the church's religious and practical functions: "Church activities in an industrial community naturally focus on social work. The world has many combinations of different kinds—one can only regret that the satisfaction of social needs has tended to deprive churches of their proper character as public buildings. Very often they are a kind of conglomeration of settlement house, youth and parish club, and parish meeting hall, with space for modest truly religious functions thrown in for good measure. The architect aimed at the full form of a church [in the Vuoksenniska plan], while seeking to provide adequately for social activities without compromises. The basic design of the church consists of a series of three consecutive halls. We may call these halls A, B, and C; A being the sanctuary proper, while the other spaces can be added if necessary by means of movable walls. On weekdays halls B and C can be used for parish activities. Each section has just under 300 seats, A and B together approximately 600, and all halls combined 800. The halls are separated by walls some 42 cm thick, sliding on a system of ball bearings in oil, and heavy enough to provide complete sound insulation. Part of the moving wall is flat, part of it is made up of cylindrical surfaces" (*Arkkitehti*, no. 12, 1959).

According to Aalto, the division of the sliding walls into flat and rounded surfaces is acoustically justified: "Divine service in a Lutheran church calls for three architectural focuses: the altar, the pulpit, and an organ loft for music and choir. All three are accommodated within a triangular form in the main church, A. As the most sacred section of the church, the altar is centrally placed, and the pulpit is generally relegated to one side. Considering that the audibility of the sermon is the most important and most difficult problem in a Lutheran church, this should logically result in an asymmetrical church interior. The long wall that diagonally faces the pulpit determines the reflection of sound to a much higher degree than the other walls. Correct design of this wall gives rise to optimum projection of sound to the congregation. In this case the acoustic wall consists of surfaces in various curved and arched forms. The whole wall, including the window surfaces, leans inward. The rounded parts of the movable walls link up with the curve of the main wall."

The division of the interior into three units gave Aalto the occasion to raise the number three into a more widely applicable, theologically justified motif: "The bell tower is dominated by the number three: its top section is tripartite, and widens upward. With this form the architect wished to create an architectural image that contrasts as strongly as possible with the factory

chimneys which dominate the surroundings. The triad recurs inside in the vault which covers the three halls. The motif converges at the altar in three unpretentious crosses. [...] The white interior has as its only accent of color a symbolic stained-glass work depicting a crown of thorns [composed by Aalto himself] in the principal windows on the west wall."

The bishop who consecrated the church took up the significance of the three crosses: they represent not only Christ alone but also the drama of Christ and the two thieves. The official name of the church is the Church of the Three Crosses.

Aalto's description can be supplemented with some technical details: the facade is of brick and concrete, rendered white; the roofing, which hangs down low on the east side, is copper sheet. The acoustic design of the vaulted interior was arrived at empirically with the help of a miniature model, in which rays of light were directed vertically and horizontally from the site of the pulpit onto small mirrors in the ceiling and walls, the premise being that sound waves are reflected in the same way as light. The inner and outer walls on the east side, between which the curved sliding walls can be pulled in, have a completely different design. The church has five entrances to ensure undisturbed separate use of the three sections, and hall A can also be used as a funeral chapel with a ceremonial exit straight to the graveyard in a beautiful pine forest setting. The basement contains a catering establishment and a mortuary on a hand-shaped plan. The vicarage southwest of the church has a wave-shaped roof ridge.

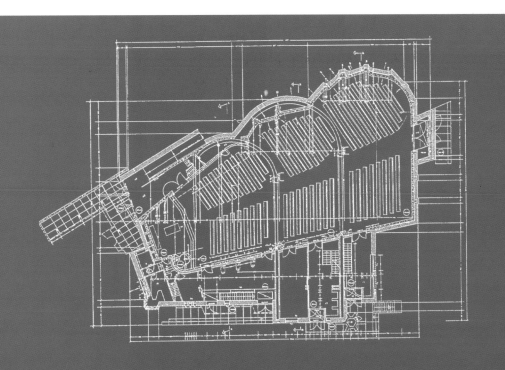

Alvar Aalto's
Studio

1956

BECAUSE OF THE INCREASE in Aalto's workload in the 1950s, the old studio at Riihitie 20 became too cramped, so in 1954 he purchased from the city a plot in Munkkiniemi, at convenient walking distance from his home. Riihitie now became his personal studio, whereas the bulk of the work was shifted to the new house. Completed in 1956, it originally consisted of a high studio wing in which he himself worked, with a diagonally placed office wing containing a workroom for a staff of 15 and a conference room on the upper floor and a little "taverna" (the architects' lunchroom) downstairs, an office, an archive room, a garage, and a small caretaker's flat. The basic idea of the white rendered brick building is the use of the angle between the two wings to produce a space that is something between a garden, a Classical theater cavea, and an open-air auditorium for lectures. The garden is cut off at the rear by the glazed long wall of the studio, shaped as a circle segment. A white concrete projection screen takes the place of a stage, and slate terraces mark rounded tiers. In 1962–63 the office section was enlarged with a new wing behind the projection screen. It contains a drafting room upstairs and a new, larger taverna downstairs, allowing the old one to be converted to administrative use. The building was purchased after Aalto's death by the Alvar Aalto Foundation, which preserves and catalogues Aalto's vast archives there, but most of the building is leased to the Alvar Aalto & Co. architectural office.

Aalto wrote about his studio: "An architect's studio should provide both peace and quiet for the individual and the possibility of group work. This is the key to the general character of the building. Turning its back on the street in almost Oriental fashion, it opens instead onto an intimate inner garden which rises, amphitheater-like, and can thus also serve as an auditorium" (*Arkkitehti*, no. 12, 1959).

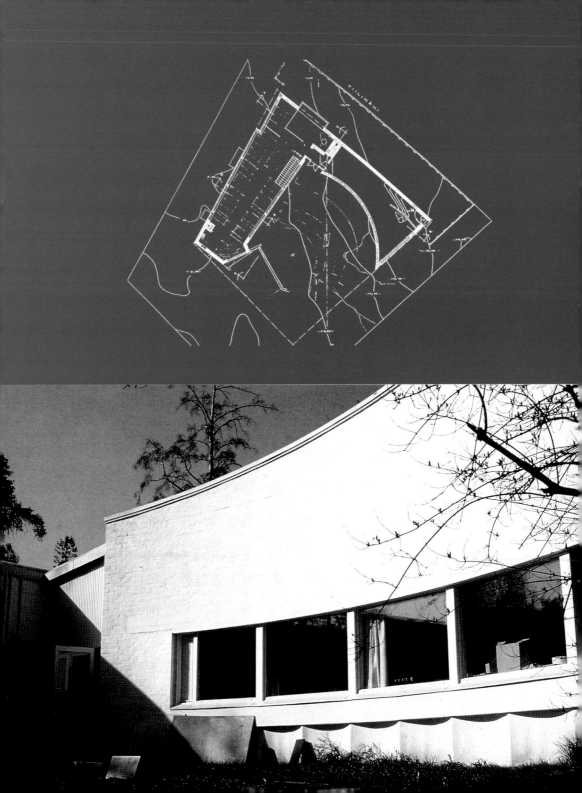

La Maison Carré 1956

AALTO WAS CONTACTED in autumn 1956 by the well-known French art dealer Louis Carré and his wife, who wished to build a villa of the highest artistic quality and material comfort on a large plot Carré had acquired near the village of Bazoches, France. The property boasts a sweeping view of a history-rich landscape that merges with the Forêt de Rambouillet. In addition to the architecture, Aalto was to be responsible for the furnishings—as exclusively designed as possible—and for the landscaping of the whole plot with terraces and plantings. He designed a house under an immense lean-to roof made of blue Normandy slate, pitched in imitation of the landscape itself. The base and parts of the walls are Chartres limestone; white rendered brick and marble were also used for the facades. Since the purpose of the house was partly to exhibit gems from the dealer's stocks to prominent clients in an exclusive domestic milieu, the rooms were divided into an entertaining section and a service section, the bedrooms being connected with the latter. The spacious entrance hall with large panels for hanging paintings has a free-form wooden ceiling, built in situ by Finnish carpenters, as was the stepped wooden ceiling of the large living room. The entire living room wall facing the view is filled by a panorama window.

Specially designed light fixtures, fixed and movable furnishings with many unique touches, complete the interior, which with its magnificent works of art rivals that of the Villa Mairea (page 46) for modern comfort. M. and Mme. Carré's separate bedrooms, connecting with a Finnish sauna and an intimate garden area sheltered from the wind, are also lavishly appointed. The rising pitch of the roof from the kitchen area, office, and the luxurious guestroom makes space for an upper story containing four staff bedrooms. The surrounding garden, with its many old trees, was landscaped by Aalto with a system of "turf stairs," i.e., low grassy terraces supported by cleft tree trunks, similar to those used in the Säynätsalo municipal offices (page 72) and Aalto's own Experimental House. The garden also contains a theater cavea built of slate, reminiscent of that enclosed by Aalto's architectural office (page 128). A garage, partly embedded into the slope, and a swimming pool complete the picture. The Maison Carré was inaugurated in 1959, but work continued until 1961. The house has been shown to the media and public only on rare occasions.

Seinäjoki Center Plan

1958

CITY AND DISTRICT centers are among the keys to Aalto's conception of architecture. The simultaneously monumental and plebeian square, with public buildings that express the personality of a town just as a person's face is an image of his inner self, occupies a central position in Aalto's world. A throwback to his early passion for antiquity, the square appears in his work occasionally as a forum (as in his plan for the new center of Helsinki, but it is also rooted in the piazza, the Italians' outdoor living room, an idea that appealed to Aalto. We find this motif for the first time in his early plan for the squares of his home town Jyväskylä, with which he hoped to promote a "New Renaissance" that, in one way or another, he continued to believe in all his life.

Aalto's *fora* or *piazze* are no sterile parading grounds bordered by lifeless props. Instead they set the stage for the ever-changing spectacle of human life; not merely for citizens' visits to public buildings but for the movements of a working day, shopping, festivals, political meetings, and an informal social life. He liked to assemble different kinds of buildings in his city centers: from city halls, churches, theaters, and libraries to shops, dance halls, restaurants, and cafés. Aalto took it as self-evident and as part of the societal responsibilities he had assumed that each of these buildings must have an architectural formulation corresponding to its functions—an individual, revealing visage of its own.

This is not to say that Aalto's city centers are outdated or romantically backward-looking. Quite the contrary: they are characterized by a highly realistic approach to the conditions prevailing in a modern, industrialized society. Bold solutions to traffic problems and the smooth adjustment of the various needs of pedestrians, cars, buses, railways, and aviation distinguish many of his center plans. He also broke away from the closed character of the traditional square in favor of an open townscape. Basically all his plans are characterized by a variety of strategies for overcoming the drawbacks of technocratic civilization. Using moderate scale and suppressing rigid geometry, providing constant reminders of or contacts with unfettered nature, giving priority to the individual, he sought to keep the forces of mechanization in check. To humanize the modern urban environment and to hearten the threatened "little man" were Aalto's goals, and for them he fought with moderation, never succumbing to a desperate hostility toward technology.

Such interest in city centers was unusual during the Rationalist years; in fact it was in direct opposition to the principles laid down in the 1933 Charte d'Athènes by the CIAM architects. No other architect in Finland was so obsessed with the monumental heart of the city. In the 1950s and '60s Aalto appeared as an out-and-out opponent to the Rationalist architecture that predominated in the Nordic countries and that was represented with particular success by his former assistant Viljo Revell.

In Seinäjoki, after the town's church council had decided to go ahead with construction of the cathedral-like church designed by Aalto in 1951 (page 90), the town council sponsored two competitions in 1958 for the planning of a monumental center in the adjacent areas. For formal reasons, Aalto did not actually win the competitions, but he received the commission. The first competition was for the area as a whole, the second had as its main theme the design of the town hall. Taking the church and the parish center that fronts it as his point of departure, Aalto

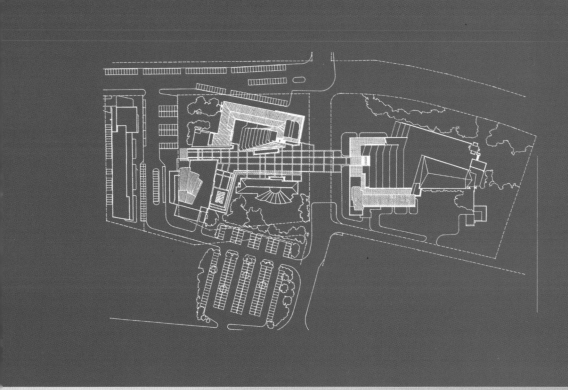

planned a unique series of coherent plazas flanked by administrative and cultural buildings. Aalto noted (page 230, volume 1 of the Artemis series on Aalto) that the center plan consists of a sequence of three squares. First comes the large court in front of the church's main entrance, which can be used as an extension of the church; second and likewise accessible to pedestrians only is the citizens' square between the town hall and library. On the short side of this oblong plaza stands the theater "alla Capella Pazzi," which functions as a backdrop like the little Brunelleschi church Aalto had admired in Florence. The third square is made up of a large star-shaped crossing to the west of the center proper, where Aalto hoped to implement his invention of "uninterrupted traffic in an intersection at grade." Beyond the theater, the center terminates in the neutral facades of the government office building. The entire complex was built step by step, including fountains, plantings, and geometric paving for pedestrian ways; the inauguration of the theater in 1987 rounded off the whole, one of Aalto's few fully realized center plans.

In the description attached to his competition entry (in the Aalto archives), Aalto wrote: "We find in the history of architecture precedents for a mere street crossing that forms the city center. Some from the period of Greek colonization have been preserved to the present day (Palermo, Quattrofontane). The four streets converging in the central point of Seinäjoki widen there, generating a liberating rhythm without, however, disrupting the interplay of building volumes. The crossing, with its widened street openings, forms a star-shaped traffic plaza, to which the pedestrian plazas are connected at the ends."

Seinäjoki
Town Hall

1958

AALTO'S PLANS FOR OFFICE buildings are just as firmly rooted in his ideas on society and life as are his cultural and religious buildings. However obvious it may seem that architecture is more impersonal than any other art form, bound up as it is with the traditions and needs of society and the wishes of clients, it is also clear that individual characteristics rooted in the designer's own preferences must creep into the work of any truly creative architect.

The town hall at Seinäjoki was built between 1963 and 1965 as the second stage (after the church) of the comprehensive city center project designed entirely by Aalto. In his plan description, Aalto wrote that he had placed the town hall as a worthy termination to the elongated entrance piazza to the church, facing the campanile at the other end. He raised the council chamber, the symbol of municipal self-government, one story above ground level on pilotis, thus creating a loggia, and turned the raised front of the chamber toward the church. As a result of his trips to Baghdad, Aalto gave the facades of the council chamber—which he originally intended to be in white rendered brick—a cladding of blue ceramic tiles, further emphasizing the building's special dignity. The town hall stands partly on an artificial hill made with earth excavated to make way for the foundations, further accentuating its monumental impact. The council chamber level thus has a secondary ground-level exit to the hill, which descends to the gardenlike citizens' square in terraces planted with flowers. The library is on one side of the square and the theater at its end. On the hill slope, Aalto imagined a series of cascades and basins; on the square he

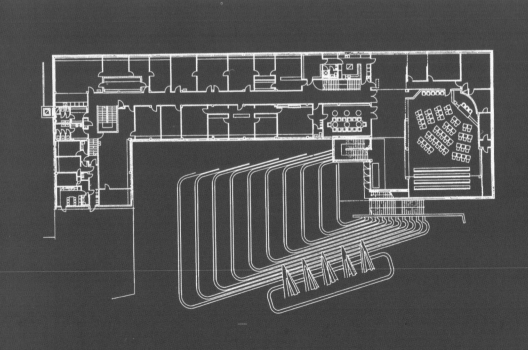

wished to have sculptures and plantings among which the city might arrange festive receptions, also using the public lobby and the town hall council chamber. The chamber is a rectangular room with visitors' benches on a level with the councillors' seats, grouped in three wedge-shaped sectors in front of the presiding officers in one corner. The steeply pitched roof is pierced by a row of "lock" skylights. Before the theater was completed, the council chamber and nearby rooms were used as the town's concert and assembly hall. Aalto designed two consecutive L-shaped wings to be built behind the council chamber; only the first of these was built. Aalto designed an annex consistent with the architecture of the previous buildings in 1973–74. This wing faces Kirkkokatu and contains offices in three stories.

Wolfsburg
Cultural Center

1958

ROOFTOP TERRACE AND SKYLIGHTS

AALTO TOOK PART IN 1958 in the invitational competition for a multipurpose building for various cultural activities in this German industrial town wholly dominated by the Volkswagen works. The designated site is next to the town hall on the main square. The center was to contain the city library, an adult education institute, and "a house of open doors," i.e., a center for hobbies and leisure activities. Aalto's entry won and was built; the center was inaugurated August 31, 1962.

Aalto's solution both linked and separated the various activities required in a highly functional way. He gave that part of the building which faces the square an air of intimate monumentality by erecting five separate, windowless auditoria, diminishing in size and clad with marble intarsia, on a column-borne arcade in a fan arrangement. The facade material is Carrara marble with vertical and horizontal bands of Pamir syenite. The main entrance is from the square beneath the auditoria and leads to the ground-floor library, the main room of which has Aalto's characteristic barrel skylights and central "book pit." A double staircase leads up from the entrance to an upper foyer with the auditoria to one side (the largest seats 238 listeners and the smallest 26; light enters only through skylight slits). On the other side is a large, open central court that can be used for open-air events. All rooms overlooking this court have glazed walls. A series of shops is located along the streetside arcade, and from the park at one of the short ends of the building one enters the "youth center" with a children's library at ground floor and club facilities, workshops for metalwork, woodwork, and pottery, table tennis rooms, a music room, etc.

Describing the plan Aalto writes: "The purpose of the cultural center was to provide psychological contrast and relaxation for this industrial town, with its monotonous working life and routine. Though roofed, the building is intended to have the same role as the agora in the cities of ancient Greece" (vol. 1 of the Artemis edition, p. 254).

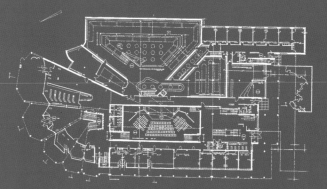

Neue Vahr
High-Rise Block

1958–62

UNLIKE MANY ARCHITECTS in former times, Aalto's calling and chief ambition was not to design castles, palaces, residences, villas, private houses, and similar buildings filled with the material comforts that are part of the lifestyle of the privileged classes. He took the great utopia of the eighteenth century, according to which every person has the right to self-fulfillment and prosperity in a democratic society, as a binding commitment. This had a particularly significant impact on his housing planning. Making sure that every citizen had the basic security provided by a decent home had in fact been the most neglected aspect of architecture in earlier times.

In 1933 Aalto wrote an article for the cultural journal *Granskaren*, in which he pointed out the connection between housing and various kinds of buildings that provide public services. In former times a whole series of functions, such as child care, primary education, and care of the sick; clothes-making and food storage; social interchange and cultural activities such as music-making, storytelling and games—not to speak of various kinds of handicrafts and paid work—took place within the home, which called for both a good deal of space and plenty of time. To varying degrees, all these functions have been largely transferred to public institutions, such as daycare centers, schools, hospitals, factories producing ready-made clothing and processed foods, laundries, dance halls, libraries, theaters, etc. The home no longer need contain everything: it can be smaller and more specialized in the basic functions of housing. Meanwhile, heating and lighting, water, and sewage systems have become more efficient and convenient.

This trend was initially hailed with undivided joy as one of the clearest proofs of progress. There were not many who realized that industrial civilization would also bring new problems and challenges. One of the first to discover the dangers was Alvar Aalto, whose insistence on humanist values and belief in the importance of individual independence opened his eyes early on to the destructive effects of Rationalism. For it is not merely housing that is rationalized and standardized by Rationalism, but equally those who are housed. The "little man" (to use a favorite expression of Aalto's) is caught somewhere between the new efficiency and the old versatility. As Aalto put it: the material slum that was once the widespread scourge of housing threatens to be replaced today by a psychological slum.

Aalto's housing design should be seen in this historical perspective. He strove to make use of the positive aspects of industrialism, the indispensable prerequisite for a more egalitarian society, but also wished to save the independence of the individual. To this end, he struggled for a scale more human than that of the industrialist anthill, with its giant factories, soulless tenement blocks, and concentration on quantity. Factories and organizations should be broken up into smaller units, with responsibility shared by a greater number of people, went Aalto's reasoning. This also means rejecting the uniformity that tends to result from mass production. Monotonous unity, sterile series of identical houses and interiors, can be avoided by means of flexible standardization.

Most important, however, is contact with living nature, a part of which man must remain if he is to preserve his physical and mental well-being. Aalto's plans for regions, towns, and districts all have contact with nature as their key theme. His basic requirement for all housing,

besides sunshine and fresh air, was constant eye contact with living nature. Whenever possible, he provided dwellings with spacious balconies, small gardens, and convenient access to nearby forests and beaches. He also surreptitiously included nature in his architectural idiom by organically grouping rooms; using free, nongeometric forms; and developing an interaction between built and natural environments.

Despite his passion for the architecture of antiquity and the Renaissance, Aalto—typically for his generation—took no interest in historical styles. He valued the buildings of the past mainly for their practical potential. They contained useful "inventions" that he was happy to make use of—but without the decorative skin. Columns, staircases of various kinds, practical connections between rooms, sheltered courtyards, linking halls, and many other items in Aalto's architectural vocabulary harked back to old models, but he used them to promote the ideal modern society that he was striving to bring about.

In practice the homes designed by Aalto provide their occupants with both individual seclusion and the opportunity for enjoyable interaction, protection from negative environmental factors and stimulation of positive ones. Financial limitations usually constrained him to design modest apartments, but he always took pains to make technology serve individualism rather than suppress it.

In 1958–62, Aalto designed a twenty-two-story apartment block that was built in a suburb of Bremen, Germany. The sketches show several variants for the building's irregular fan plan. Built of prefabricated bituminous concrete blocks, the house contains nine small apartments per story; there are no apartments on the ground floor. The main feature is a large living room opening out in a V-shaped sector to a wholly glazed wall and a balcony facing west and screened off from the neighbors. This enables the residents to enjoy maximum daylight while at home. Elevators, stairwells, and airing balconies are on the narrow east side. The building was intended for "social-collective living," which is why each story has a common room, a kind of collective living room. The roof story has a club locale and a covered viewing terrace. The ground floor contains a free-form hall with an office and small shops for residents. Pedestrians have direct access to the district's central square and to the house parking.

Opera and
Music Theater

1959

FOR THIS BUILDING in Essen, Germany, Aalto took part in the invitational competition in 1959. He won first prize, and went on reworking the plan at the city building committee's behest from 1961 right up to his death. From 1970 to 1976 his German collaborator was Bauasessor Horst Loy; the opera house was finally built between 1981 and 1988 under the supervision of the German architect Harald Deilmann, mainly on the basis of drawings left by Aalto.

The basic plan remained unaltered throughout. The opera house contains a large, asymmetrical auditorium with seating for a total of some 1,100 spectators, partly on the sloping parquet and partly on three rows of balconies with serpentine fronts leaning inward in an effect related to that of Aalto's "Northern Lights" wall in the New York World's Fair pavilion (page 44). The functional gain was that the distance to the stage for the spectators sitting highest up was the same as for those in the lowest balcony rows. The side walls, which point toward the stage, are clad with a system of bent battens (originally to have been laminated wood, but because of the danger of fire eventually made of aluminum), which have both an acoustic and an aesthetic function. The ceiling, with a system of metal netting that is permeable by sound waves but hidden from sight, conceals an "echo chamber" above with movable acoustic screens producing the "flexible acoustics" that Aalto had so long sought to implement in various ways. Behind the auditorium, and equal to it in height, is the foyer, with open, sinuous entrance galleries to the balconies forming an upward-growing light court—a mirror image to the auditorium. As in the Helsinki House of Culture (page 104), Aalto mirrors the forms of these principal spaces in the

CAFÉ IM THEATER

exterior: the walls curve softly, and the whole massive structure is covered by a lean-to roof that takes a low step up above the auditorium and stage. The building stands free in a park.

The variation between successive plans was partly due to financially dictated, alternate enlargements and cuts. Thus, a studio stage for 250 spectators was ultimately scrapped. Aalto planned to use white Carrara marble for the facades, but because of air pollution finally settled for dark cast aluminum. Fortunately, however, before construction got under way, a granite that was light enough to produce the originally intended effect was found. Technical improvements also made the "acoustically flexible" ceiling a success, which was not the case in the Finlandia Hall (page 198). The final, purely aesthetic equilibrium of forms and proportions that was so important to Aalto's works, however, was partly lost in the "hard," engineerlike implementation; thus, to some extent, the Essen Opera House lacks the aura of a genuine Aalto work.

Aalto's description of the competition entry states: "The purpose of the auditorium's asymmetrical form is that the house will not seem empty even with smaller audiences. It also produces a longer wall for the loges... The deep blue (indigo) walls of the auditorium contrast with the white marble gallery fronts" (vol. 1 of the Artemis edition, p. 250).

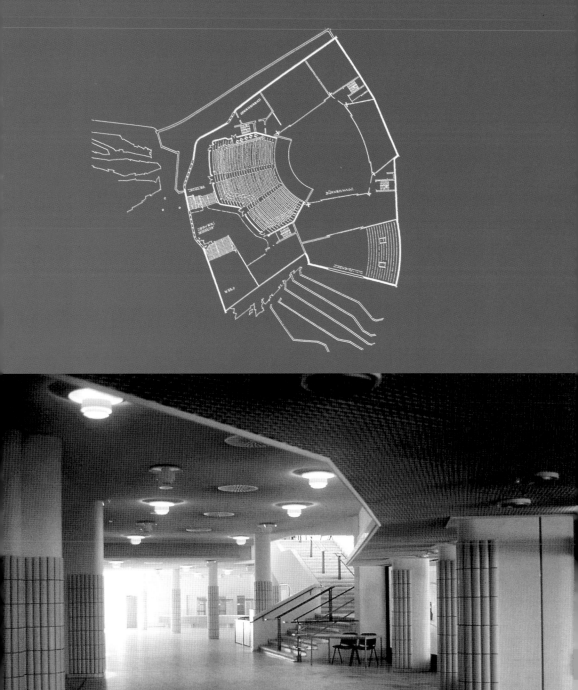

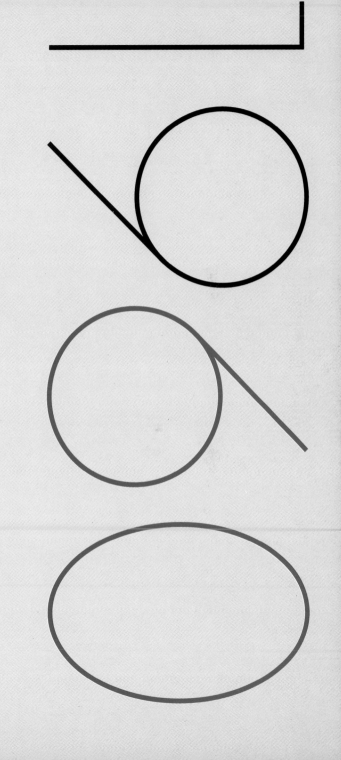

Seinäjoki
City Library

1960–65

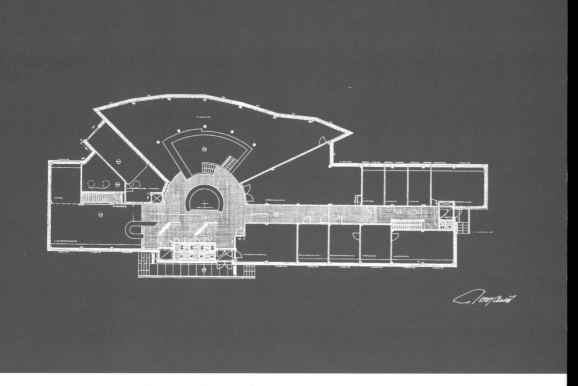

AS DESCRIBED UNDER the Seinäjoki center plan competitions (page 144), Aalto designated a site for a future library on the south side of the promenade square, flanked by the town hall on the north side and the theater on the west. The earliest sketches show a rectangular library building with a fan-shaped auditorium at one end and a wedge-shaped storeroom for books along the south side. When elaborating the final plans between 1960 and 1965, Aalto altered the form of the library completely. The core of the new plan is an asymmetrical, fan-shaped lending and stack room, which breaks out of the south end of the longish, rectangular building in a raised, wing-shaped section. The lending and control desk is at the center of the fan; next to it is a small "book pit" with stacks and reading tables. From a round colonnade surrounding the lending counter, the ceiling arches up toward the high window front in the south facade. A series of horizontal screens outside filters the sunlight; elsewhere the building has strip windows superimposed with vertical, white-painted trelliswork. Separate from the main room are a children's section, a reference section with study desks, conference rooms, and offices. The basement contains the archives and a garage for a mobile library that distributes books to rural areas. The exterior is whitewashed. The library was inaugurated in 1965.

Seinäjoki City Theater

1961

AMONG THE CULTURAL BUILDINGS that Aalto designed, he felt most at home with theaters, concert halls, cinemas, libraries, and museums. These are the mainstays of the individual's quest and growth; the gateways to true freedom of culture and to lofty visions. In these institutions, genera- tion after generation encounters the forerunners who have created, over the millennia, our common cultural heritage and its monuments which, though products of a specific time and place, are enduring and universal. With such monuments, also, we can make our own contribution to the conquests of the human spirit during our brief sojourn on earth. To provide suitable and worthy settings for such activities was, to Aalto, the most significant and most inspiring task of the architect. Here he raised veritable temples to his humanist credo.

The cinemas and theaters designed by Aalto in the 1920s and '30s generally formed part of building complexes with other functions besides the theatrical one. His theater auditorium—or, to be precise, assembly hall—in the Jyväskylä Workers' Club (page 16) followed the conventions common to most workers' club and youth club buildings at the time. Aalto gave the theater in the Agricultural Cooperative Building a tiered, symmetrical auditorium, programmatically diverging from the theaters with stalls and galleries erected by the old class society.

In Aalto's 1952 competition plan for the Kuopio Theater we find for the first time the asymmetrical auditorium that featured in all his later theater and concert hall plans. From then on, he gave his theaters a sculptural design, arranging the entire building around an asymmetrical auditorium, thus creating cultural landmarks. The theaters built by other architects in Finland during the 1950s, '60s, and '70s tend to lack the free form and resulting expressivity of Aalto's theaters.

Aalto's competition entry for Seinäjoki center also indicated the location and approximate form of the future theater house. Detailed planning of the theater began in 1961. Initially Aalto had in mind a free-form auditorium for 348 spectators within straight external walls, but his final plan from 1968–69 provided a flexible solution to the problem of size, with space for an audience of 400 in the asymmetrical main auditorium; a further 150 can be seated by removing the sliding wall that separates the main auditorium from a side auditorium and connecting the rows of seats. The smaller room can also be used separately for lectures or concerts. Only after Aalto's death, however, did Seinäjoki decide to carry out this last link in the original center plan. The final design, drawn up by the Aalto office under Elissa Aalto and built in 1984–87, was based on the earlier plan, but omitted the small auditorium. The theater has a large entrance-level hall containing a cloakroom desk in free form and a café with 120 seats. The foyer is on the upper floor, and leads to the downward-sloping auditorium for 429 spectators. The auditorium and stage rise out from the main body of the building, forming a superstructure clad in copper that contrasts with the white ceramic tiles used for the remaining facades. The theater was inaugurated in 1987.

Rovaniemi City Library

1961–66

DESIGNED IMMEDIATELY AFTER the Seinäjoki Library (page 180), the Rovaniemi City Library develops some of the earlier building's themes on a both broader and more detailed scale. The planning was done between 1961 and 1966; construction took place from 1965 to 1968. In addition to a considerably larger collection of books for a larger readership, the building had to accommodate several special departments. The fan-shaped lending and stack section has the strongest claim to being the main room. It protrudes from the main building mass on the piazza side; here, too, is the main entrance that leads to a long entrance hall with access to the lending area, a newspaper room, a space for temporary exhibitions, and a section containing stuffed arctic birds. A staircase leads down to the geological museum, music library, and archives below. The raised facade of the lending room faces the central square; divided into five crystal-like, projecting sectors, it is clad with white, vertical ceramic tiles, and crowned with glazed "lock skylights" that provide the lending room with shadowless lighting. The wall sectors open outward, fanlike, providing a striking frame for the stack circle and central lending desk. The plan structure is repeated in the "book pits" sunk into the floor, containing those books that are not lent out, with stairs leading further down to the basement archives. Trapezoidal reading desks in the book pits and on the main level are for visitors' use. In addition to the large lock skylights on the piazza side, several smaller ones are spread about the building, forming motifs developed from the exhibition pavilion in Venice and the Aalborg Museum. The first link in Aalto's plan for the town's new center to be carried out, carefully studied in every detail, architecturally lavish, the Rovaniemi Library is a building of exceptional formal balance.

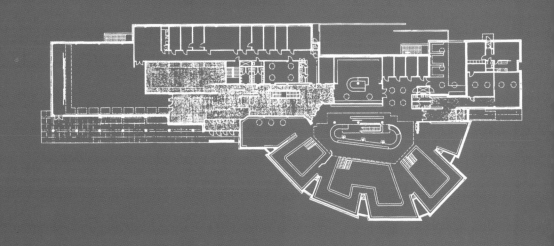

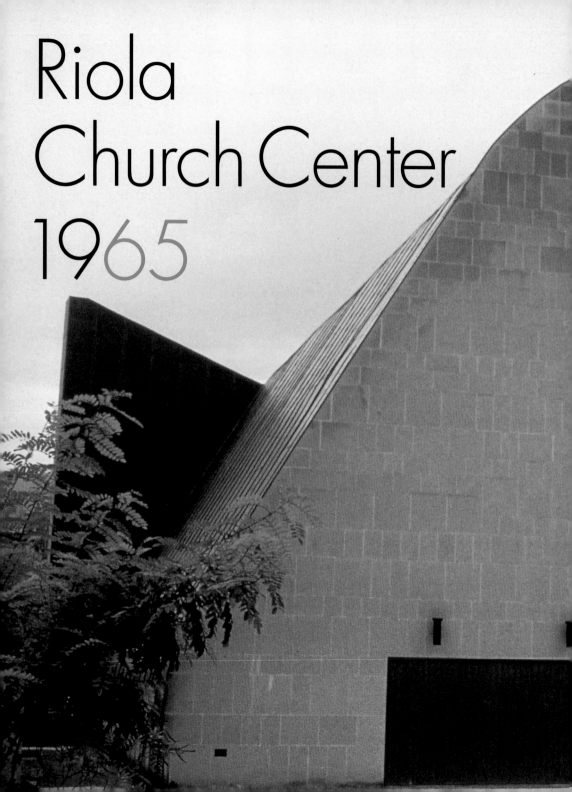

Riola
Church Center
1965

THE SMALL ITALIAN MOUNTAIN village of Riola di Verga lies on a slope of the Apennines some 40 kilometers south of Bologna along the road to Pistoia. The ecumenically inclined Bishop of Bologna, Cardinal Giacomo Lercaro, asked Aalto in 1965 to design a small church next to the old highway bridge across the river Reno. Aalto's initial plan from 1966 already showed the church in its final form, but it was later supplemented by more comprehensive but unrealized plans for an old people's home and a kindergarten. Planning resumed in 1969 and again in 1975, continuing until 1980.

As in Seinäjoki (page 90), Aalto laid out an enclosed piazza in front of the church in order to enable a congregation of thousands to participate in divine services at major religious festivals. He also thought that the church itself, which normally seats a congregation of 200, could be divided by a gigantic sliding wall into a mini-church—comprising the altar, chancel, and baptistry—and a larger room for nonreligious events. The plan is an asymmetrical, slightly wedge-shaped basilica with an unusual roof system consisting of stepped, longitudinal vault fragments inclined toward the chancel. The vertical surfaces of the vaults are glazed, so that the whole church is bathed in light reflected by the white vaults. The vault system, which rises at ground level from one of the long walls, is borne by seven gently curved, asymmetrical concrete arches, related in form to Aalto's wood furniture. The baptistry is on a somewhat lower level to the right of the chancel; it has a lantern visible from outside and a window overlooking the river below. A campanile consisting of five parallel vertical concrete planks rises on the far side of the forecourt, providing an optical lift to the inclined roof of the church. One of the forecourt's long sides is walled off from the river ravine, the other is lined by a colonnade and a modest parish building with youth clubs, meeting rooms, etc. To the left of the chancel is the vestry, which forms part of the vicar's apartment. For a site some way off Aalto designed a *casa di riposo* (old people's home) with cafeteria and a *scuola materna* (kindergarten).

Financial problems delayed implementation, and the church center finally built between 1975 and 1980 was merely a shadow of the original plan. The most regrettable omission was that of the campanile, quite indispensable for the overall impression; the deletion of the forecourt, the riverside terraces, and the vicar's residence also left unfortunate gaps. The movable wall in the church interior was replaced by a mere drapery, which in no way justifies the mighty "wing" that projects from one side of the roof, a relic of the intended sliding wall. The old people's home and kindergarten were not built.

Finlandia
Hall

1962

IN 1962 THE HELSINKI CITY authorities commissioned Aalto to design a concert and congress building as the first part of his great center plan. Finlandia Hall was completed nine years later. Even the earliest plans show the main characteristics of the final solution (the main drawings are dated May 10, 1967). The most conspicuous alterations involved the facade treatment (initially a fine pattern of stone intarsia) and the chamber music room, originally intended to soar like the main auditorium above the main building mass.

Finlandia Hall was adapted strictly to Aalto's center plan, with its main (eastern) facade turned toward the projected Terrace Square and the car entrance on the bottom level, intended to continue in the form of a tunnel to other cultural buildings along the shore of Töölö Bay. At this level each section's own access stair can be reached by car. The next story, or entrance level, with doors opening directly into Hesperia Park, is dominated by the entrance hall, and also contains cloakrooms and other service space. A broad "Venetian" staircase leads up to the foyers with entrances to the large and small auditorium, the restaurant, etc. Smaller Venetian staircases (one of which forms a visible exterior motif in the east facade) lead from the main foyer to the gallery-like balcony foyer and the doors to the main auditorium's balcony. The small chamber music room, which has adjustable, shield-shaped acoustic screens attached to the ceiling, seats 350 people; the main auditorium seats 1,750.

In Finlandia Hall, Aalto produced variations on some of the key ideas for the Essen Opera House (page 174), including asymmetry, acoustic wall sculptures, and the contrast of cobalt blue walls with the white marble of the gallery front. This consoled him somewhat for the constant postponements of the German project. For the Essen Opera, however, the delay turned out to be a blessing, as two mistakes made in building the Finlandia Hall were avoided when construction finally got under way in 1987. These were the use of fragile Carrara marble for the facades, later necessitating a costly renovation, and the large "echo chamber" for variable acoustics (the true reason for the Finlandia Hall's proud, obliquely cut crown). It turned out that the entire louvered ceiling between the two spaces had to be sealed off for the main auditorium's acoustics to work at all. In Essen the echo chamber functions in the intended way owing to a better design of the louvered ceiling.

Finlandia Hall was inaugurated in December 1971. Planning of a congress section began even before the main wing was completed; the congress wing was ready for use as early as 1975. The idea was to improve the working conditions for conferences, an important aspect of the building's use. The annex turned out to be a boon in 1975, when the Conference on Security and Cooperation in Europe (CSCE) brought the heads of state of 32 nations to Helsinki, and the subsequently oft-cited Helsinki Declaration was signed at Finlandia Hall. The congress wing, linked to the south end of the main building, contains a large foyer, conference rooms of various sizes, and two large congress halls that seat a combined total of 900 delegates and are wired to glass booths for simultaneous interpreters, TV, radio, the press, etc. The west facade of the wing has large windows and rounded, concave hollows to make space for some of the old trees growing on the site—and to enliven the facade. Despite the mistakes made in construction, Finlandia Hall ranks as one of the artistic high-water marks in Aalto's career.

Mount Angel Benedictine Abbey Library 1964–67

THE DIRECTORS OF THE Benedictine abbey's seminary, in Oregon, asked Aalto in 1964 to design a library building in the midst of the older educational and religious buildings that enclose the seminary campus on a hilltop surrounded by rural countryside. Aalto visited the site in 1967 shortly before construction was to begin, but it was too late for him to do anything about the plan's principal weakness, which was that the library blocks the view from the last vantage point on the campus. What appealed to him about the assignment was the sharply sloping terrain, which allowed him to give full expression to his idea of the "book pit." The entire library is one gigantic book pit that descends from the campus-level entrace to two fan-shaped landings. The lending desk at the center of the fan is surrounded by a curved clerestory skylight that provides shadowless light to the landings on three levels and to the connecting staircases. The reading areas are placed within reach of the light court. The books are in stacks radiating toward the periphery, lit by by further "lock skylights" and strip windows placed high up in the curved, four-part facade. Small carrels are placed along the window wall of the lower level. The basement level, containing the archives, also has high strip windows facing the slope. The main level at the top houses a lobby, various technical facilities and offices, a large auditorium with obliquely placed tiers, and a room for rest or meditation—the only lookout spot with an extensive view. The older school buildings flanking the library are connected to it by a pergola. The facade material is rough yellow brick, the roofing is copper sheet, and much use of Oregon pine was made in the interiors. The building, inaugurated in 1968, was donated to the abbey by Jean and Howard Vollum.

Fu

C

rniture
and
bjects

Furniture with Otto Korhonen

1928

IT IS NO COINCIDENCE that Aalto first made his international breakthrough as a furniture designer, or that his furniture continues to be used for new interiors—its popularity shows no sign of flagging, although a whole generation has passed since he perfected the design of his best-known models. His furniture design was one of his foremost achievements in its own right, and in many cases it sowed the seed from which his architectural ideas sprang forth.

Through furniture Aalto came into direct contact with a natural material—living wood—which offered him the sensory resistance and concrete results that the abstractions he dealt with on his desk could not provide. Referring to his bentwood furniture, he spoke of wishing to learn "the language of wood fibers." The lesson was so important that occasionally he made even brick and concrete speak the language of wood; for him this was nature's own language. An early example is the centrally placed bearing column in the round assembly hall of the Seinäjoki Defense Corps Building (page 12). Its downward-tapering form is not a loan from Minoan architecture, as some critics have asserted: Igor Herler conclusively proved that it is a furniture leg translated to a monumental scale. Later examples of wood forms transferred to architecture are the free serpentine shapes that occur so frequently in Aalto's architecture (starting with the Paimio Sanatorium's solarium balconies and entrance canopy [page 18]) and the open fan, one of his favorite architectural motifs, derived from the ramification of a growing tree.

Aalto's early Neoclassicism, in which he playfully varied and combined forms from historicist repertory, also found its first full-fledged expression in furniture design, as in the extravagant furnishings of the Seurahuone café in Jyväskylä and the Hämäläis-Osakunta student

union locale in Helsinki—both dating from 1924, before he had had the chance to put the principle of mixed styles into architectural practice in the Jyväskylä Workers' Club (page 16) and Muurame Church.

From 1928, when Aalto embarked on a long-standing collaboration with the experienced master joiner Otto Korhonen and his Turku company Huonekalu-ja rakennustyötehdas. Their first joint effort was a stackable wooden chair invented by Korhonen and improved by Aalto. This was the standard chair used for the Jyväskylä Defense Corps Building's auditorium. Aalto also designed a stackable armchair with a pronounced Art Nouveau look. Both pieces were exhibited in summer 1929 in a pavilion designed by Aalto for displaying the joinery firm's products at the Turku 700th-century exhibition. Also exhibited was a bedroom suite which included a chair that was the forerunner of all of Aalto's later bentwood furniture, with the seat and back made of a single, gently curving piece of plywood. Aalto learned the technique of molding wood from Korhonen, who soon found himself with Aalto on the cutting edge of a complex process of technological development.

AALTO'S FIRST CHAIR WITH MOLDED ONE-PIECE SEAT AND BACK, 1929

Furniture in the Bauhaus Style

1928

IN 1928 AALTO ordered some of Marcel Breuer's "Wassily" armchairs and a number of Breuer's cantilevered tubular steel chairs, which he admired for being made by industrial mass production methods. His own bedroom chair, shown at the Turku exhibition, had a seat and back made industrially but legs crafted manually. In 1929 Aalto and Korhonen started to experiment with combinations of their own molded plywood seats and Breuer's tubular steel bases. The result was a kind of "hybrid chair" that combined wood and tubular steel as materials in a completely industrialized production process. In 1931 Sigfried Giedion's Zurich furniture company Wohnbedarf started carrying a stackable version of the hybrid chair with a springy base as well as an easy-to-convert tubular steel sofabed.

As a result of his friendship with Laszlo Moholy-Nagy, whom he first met in 1930, Aalto adopted the Bauhaus method of experimenting with forms and materials in a quest for new ways to develop utility articles. Aalto and Korhonen started making reliefs of birch plies bent in gentle curves, producing abstract sculptures of sorts, which Aalto used as an instructive accompaniment to his furniture exhibitions, including the event that marked the international breakthrough for his new furniture models, the London exhibition of 1933. The design feats of the Paimio chair in 1931—a companion piece, made entirely of laminated and molded plywood, to Breuer's Wassily armchair—and the "Chair 31," a cantilevered wooden armchair (1932), were directly connected with his experiments with wood. Another step forward was the L-shaped furniture leg (1933) fastened with screws to a horizontal top. The first extensive application of the L leg was in the low-backed chairs for Viipuri Library, but its most widespread use was for the round, stackable, three-legged stool, millions of which have been sold.

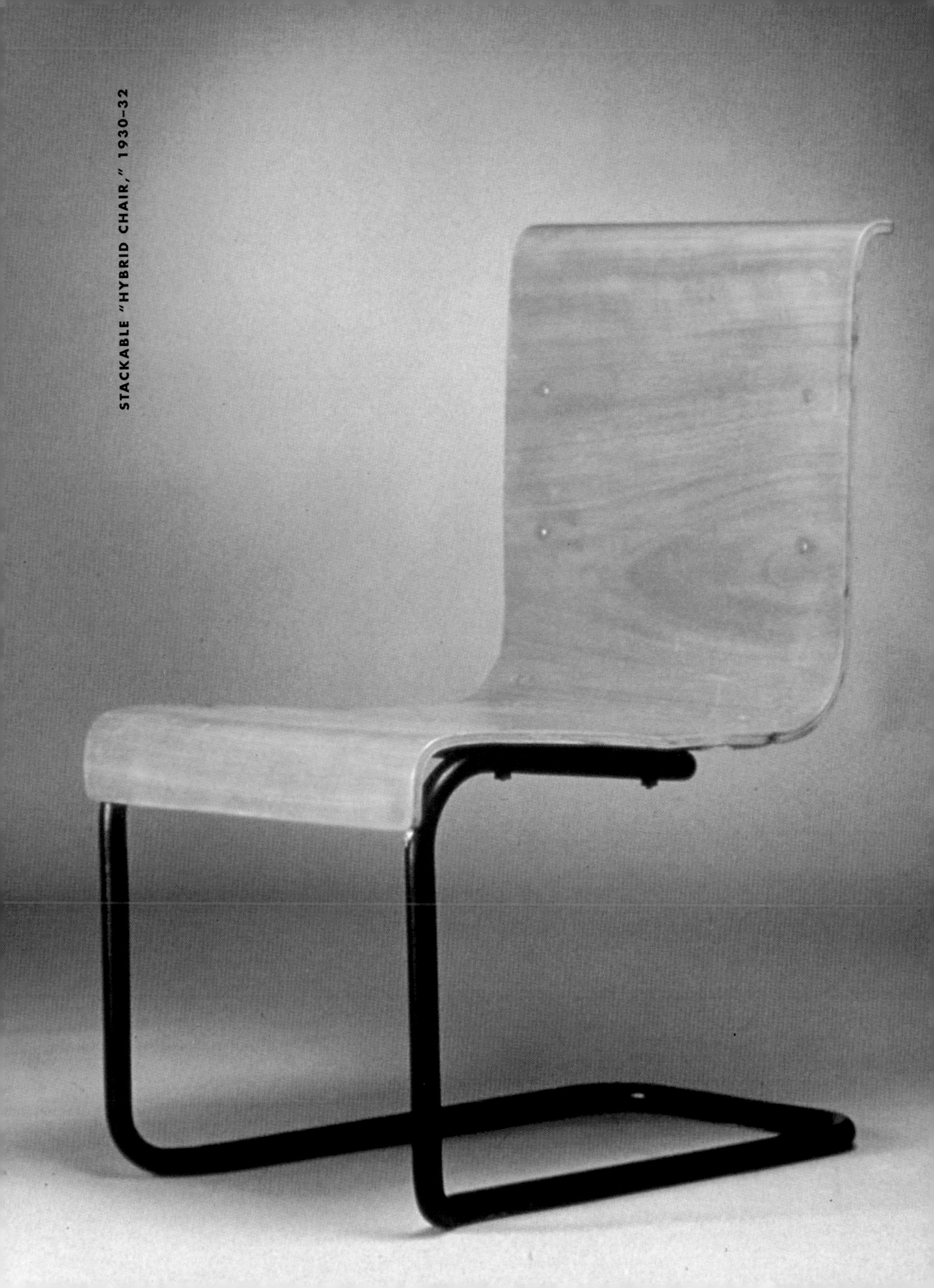

STACKABLE "HYBRID CHAIR," 1930–32

Furniture by Artek

1935

LIVELY DEMAND for Aalto furniture following the 1933 exhibition in London led to the founding of Artek in 1935. The company's main task was (and still is) to supply the international and domestic markets with Aalto furniture made at the Korhonen factory in Turku. The company was supervised by Aalto until his death, but attained fairly independent status in producing variations of and additions to Aalto's original models. This was partly because Aino Aalto assumed a leading role in Artek from the beginning, and also because other members of the Artek team, such as the gifted furniture designer Maija Heikinheimo, identified themselves so fully with Aalto's goals that their products were spontaneously "Aaltoesque."

Aalto called the furniture leg "the little sister of the column," as its form gave rise to a number of stylistic variants. The laminated, molded, right-angled L leg, patented in 1933, originated the three-legged stool as well as chairs with a backrest, cantilevered chairs and armchairs, and more. During the war, when the glue needed for the process was not available, Artek developed Aalto's idea of garden tables and chairs held together by wire. In 1946 he created prototype furniture using the "Y" leg, which consists of two L bends placed at an angle. In 1954 he designed the "X" leg, a fan-shaped transition from bearing to borne member. He tested a series of ideas for joining leg and seat, including metal sockets and spaghetti-like molded wooden "strings." One might speak of a special Aalto furniture style, unaffected, pleasantly tactile, of vigorous proportions and harmonious forms, created by the master though he did not personally design all variants.

AALTO CALLED THE
FURNITURE LEG
"THE LITTLE SISTER
OF THE COLUMN."

Karhula-Iittala Glass Design

1936

AALTO'S INTEREST IN OBJECTS for the home was aroused early: he joined Ornamo, the Finnish Association of Designers, in 1920. He did not, however, have the opportunity to concentrate on glass design until 1932, partly because he lived far from Finland's design centers and partly because unfavorable economic trends reduced the Finnish glassworks to passivity at the time. The controversial Functionalist exhibition in Stockholm in 1930 sparked considerable interest in modern industrial art for the general public in Finland, too. This led to a series of design competitions for glass objects and paved the way for the heroic years of Finnish design in the 1930s. Both Alvar and Aino Aalto took part in these competitions, in which their international orientation and faithfulness to the idiom of avant-garde art brought them unexpected success despite their lack of specialized experience.

An interesting point about their entries is that the contrast in their temperament and artistic outlook, which the closeness of their collaboration in architectural projects makes difficult to pin down, appears clearly in their glass designs, in which they were in open rivalry. Aino's strength was on the practical, everyday, programmatically social plane, whereas Alvar followed his artistic demon; they both achieved results of enduring high quality. Aino's pressed drinking glasses and jugs are widespread utility ware in Finland today; Alvar's "Savoy" vase is the internationally best-known Finnish design object. The vase can actually be taken as a symbol of Aalto's whole life's work and relationship to nature, since it is related equally to his experimental wood reliefs, to his furniture, and to the organic structures which characterize his buildings.

Before the 1937 World's Fair in Paris, for which Aalto had designed the Finnish pavilion

(page 42), the glassworks announced a design competition. Entries were to comprise a minimum of five objects. Aalto's entry, "Eskimåerindens skinnbuxa" (The Eskimo Woman's Leather Breech), showed free-form glass objects with sinuous contours drawn in crayon on varicolored bits of cardboard and sketch paper. The effect was strikingly similar to modern collage art. The design, completely unconventional and technologically unproven, was boldly awarded first prize by the jury, and the first samples of what was later known (incorrectly) as the "Savoy vase," and of its variants, were blown in wooden molds that gradually burned away. As a result of the shrewdly formulated competition program, the glassworks never had to pay royalties for the hundreds of thousands of objects made to the winning design.

CHRONOLOGICAL LIST OF AALTO'S MAJOR WORKS

Only the year when planning began is indicated. The sign * indicates projects fully or partly realized.

1919
Alajärvi youth association building*

1920
Elementary school for Kauhajärvi*

1921
Kauhajärvi bell tower and church*

1922
Second Finnish trade fair in Tampere*

1923
Restoration of Toivakka Church*
Chief Constable Karpio's summer villa, Jyväskylä*
Nuora House, Jyväskylä*
Terho Manner's house, Töysä*
Competition entry for the Finnish Parliament House

1924
Alajärvi Municipal Hospital*
Seinäjoki Defense Corps Building*
Jyväskylä Workers' Club*
Railway officials' block of flats, Jyväskylä*
Furnishing of the Seurahuone Café, Jyväskylä*

1925
Renovation of Kemijärvi Church*
Renovation of Korpilahti Church*
Pertunmaa Church
Funeral Chapel for Jyväskylä
Competition entry for Jämsä Church
Perniö Museum
"Casa Laurén," Jyväskylä*
"Atrium House," Alajärvi

1926
Competition entry for Jyväskylä vicarage
Jyväskylä Defense Corps Building*
Competition entry for the Union Bank Building, Helsinki
"Villa Flora," Alajärvi*
Town plan for Sammallahti, Jämsä municipality
Sketches for the Palais des Nations, Geneva, Switzerland
Muurame Church*

1927
Officials' housing for Wilh. Schauman company, Joensuu*
Competition entry for health spa in Pärnu, Estonia
Competition entry for Viipuri City Library
Competition entry for Töölö Church, Helsinki
Competition entry for SW Finland Agricultural Coop.
　　Building, Turku*
Competition entry and project for Taulumäki Church, Jyväskylä
Competition entry for Viinikka Church, Tampere
Competition entry for Kinkomaa tuberculosis sanatorium
Standard apartment block, the Tapani Building, Turku*

1928
Suomen Biografi cinema in Turku
Turun Sanomat building, Turku*
Three standard houses in the Aitta summerhouse competition
Competition entry for Paimio tuberculosis sanatorium*
Competition entry for an Independence Monument in Helsinki
Competition entry for a lighthouse in the Dominican Republic
Furniture developed jointly with Otto Korhonen*

1929
Competition entry for Kälviä tuberculosis sanatorium
Competition entry for Vallila Church, Helsinki
City of Turku 700th anniversary exhibition*

1930
ToppilaVaara pulp mill, Oulu*
Competition entry for Turku water tower
Competition entry for Vierumäki Sports Institute
Competition entry for Tehtaanpuisto Church, Helsinki
Competition entry for the G.A. Serlachius company
　　headquarters, Mänttä
Sets for pacifist play on Turku Finnish Theater*
Furnishing of living room, bedroom and kitchen at the Minimum
Apartment Exhibition in the Helsinki Art Hall*

1931
Competition entry for enlargement of the University of Helsinki
Competition entry for Zagreb central hospital, Yugoslavia
Competition entries for Lallukka artists' home

1932
Fanshaped sauna, Paimio*
Competition entry for EnsoGutzeit weekend cottage
Villa Tammekann, Tartu, Estonia*
Karhulalittala glass design competition*

1933
Entry in the ideas competition for Nedre Norrmalm, Stockholm
Competition entry for Temppeliaukio Church in Helsinki
Entry in the first competition for Helsinki Stadium
Entry in the final competition for Helsinki Stadium
Viipuri City Library, final version*

1934
Competition entry for Helsinki Fair Hall
Competition entry for Tampere railway station
Competition entry for Helsinki main post office
Town plan for Munkkiniemi, Helsinki
Highrise housing area in Munkkiniemi, Helsinki

1935
Kalastajatorppa restaurant in Munkkiniemi, Helsinki
Aalto's own home and office in Munkkiniemi, Helsinki*
Competition entry for Finnish Legation building in Moscow, Russia

1936
Competition entry for the central warehouse of the State alcohol
　　monopoly in Helsinki
Competition entry for the Finnish pavilion at the 1937 World's Fair
　　in Paris*
Karhulalittala glass design competition*
Master plan and housing for Varkaus*
Master plan, pulp mill and housing for Sunila, Kotka*

1937

Competition entry for an extension to the Helsinki University Library
Competition entry for Tallinn Art Museum, Estonia
Master plan and housing for Karhula*
Nordic Union Bank branch office in Karhula*
Master plan, paper mill and housing for Inkeroinen*
Weekend house for Mr Richmond Temple
Furnishing of the Savoy restaurant in Helsinki*

1938

Master plan and housing for Kauttua*
Inkeroinen elementary school*
Villa Mairea, Noormarkku*
Three competition entries for the Finnish pavilion at the 1939
   World's Fair in New York*
"Forest pavilion" for the Agricultural Exhibition at Lapua*
Film studio for Erik Blomberg in Westend, Espoo
Jalasjärvi Defense Corps building
Aalto exhibition at the Museum of Modern Art in New York*

1940

HAKA construction company's competition for housing in Helsinki
"An American town" in Finland
AA System standardized houses*
"Village of comrades in arms" in Tampere*

1941

Regional plan for the Kokemäenjoki river valley*
A. Ahlström Oy head office in Varkaus
Entrance to bomb shelter at Erottaja, Helsinki*

1942

Master plan and lowrise housing for Säynätsalo*
Competition entry for Merikoski power plant, Oulu
Villa Tvistbo near Ludvika, Sweden

1943

Town plan for the Oulu riverside, the "River Rapids Center"
Master plan for the Strömberg company's industrial estate and
   housing in Vaasa*
Master plan for Nynäshamn, Sweden*

1944

Johnson Institute in Avesta, Sweden
Town center of Avesta
"Reindeer horn plan" for Rovaniemi*
Sauna in Kauttua*

1945

"Negro village" in Huutoniemi, Vaasa*
Competition entry for Nynäshamn Town Hall

1946

Artek pavilion in Hedemora, Sweden*
Heimdal housing area in Nynäshamn, Sweden
Villa Kauppi in Hirvisalo near Heinola*
Senior Dormitory, MIT, Cambridge, Massachusetts*

1947

Master plan of Imatra*
Villa Kihlman on Lake Näsijärvi*
Aino and Alvar Aalto exhibition in Helsinki, celebrating 25 years
   of collaboration*

1948

Competition entry for the National Pensions Institute in Helsinki
Finnish Engineering Society building in Helsinki*
Säynätsalo municipal offices*

1949

Town planning competition for Otaniemi, Espoo*
Competition entry for a passenger terminal in Helsinki

1950

Regional plan for the province of Lapland
Indoor stadium on the campus of Otaniemi, Espoo*
Competition entry for Lahti Church
Competition for a chapel in Malmi graveyard, Helsinki
Competition entry for Kivelä hospital in Helsinki

1951

Area plan, factory and housing for Typpi Oy, Oulu*
Competition entry for Seinäjoki Church*
Competition entry for Glostrup hospital, Copenhagen, Denmark
Competition entry for Jyväskylä Institute of Pedagogics
   (later Jyväskylä University)*
"Rautatalo" commercial building in Helsinki*
Country club for EnsoGutzeit Oy in Kallahti, Helsinki*

1952

Competition entry for a funeral chapel and cemetery in Lyngby
   Taarbaek, Denmark
Competition entry for Kuopio Theater
National Pensions Institute office in Helsinki*
Experimental house on Muuratsalo island, Säynätsalo*
House of Culture, Helsinki*

1953

Helsinki University of Technology main building, Otaniemi*
National Pensions Institute housing in Munkkiniemi, Helsinki*
Competition for sports, concerts, etc. complex at Vogelweidplatz,
   Vienna, Austria

1954

Master plan, paper mill and housing for EnsoGutzeit Oy in Summa*
Alvar Aalto's studio in Munkkiniemi, Helsinki*
Apartment block in the Hansaviertel, Berlin, Germany*
Central Finland Museum in Jyväskylä*
The motor boat "Nemo prophetia in patria"*

1955

Villa Sambonet in a Milan suburb, Italy
Competition entry for the National Bank head office, Baghdad, Iraq
Theater and concert hall in Oulu
Competition for municipal offices in Gothenburg, Sweden
Finnish pavilion in Venice's biennale park, Italy*
Church of The Three Crosses at Vuoksenniska, Imatra*
Housing and business complex "Sundh Center" in Avesta, Sweden*
Typpi Oy site manager's house "Villa Lehmus" in Oulu*

1956
Competition entry for main railway station in Gothenburg, Sweden
La Maison Carré in Bazoches, France*
Korkalovaara housing area in Rovaniemi*
Plan for University of Oulu campus

1957
Town plan and housing for Kampementsbacken in Stockholm
Competition entry for town hall in Marl, Germany
Art Museum in Baghdad, Iraq
General Post Office in Baghdad, Iraq

1958
Wolfsburg Cultural Center, Germany*
North Jutland Art Museum in Aalborg, Denmark*
Competition entry for Kiruna Town Hall, Sweden*
"Neue Vahr" highrise block in Bremen, Germany*
Munkkiniemi youth center, Helsinki

1959
Opera house and music theater in Essen, Germany*
Town plan and housing for Karhusaari and Hanasaari islands, Espoo
EnsoGutzeit Oy headquarters, Helsinki*
Plans for the new center of Helsinki
Memorial to the battle of Suomussalmi, sculpture*
Power plant at the Lieksankoski rapids*

1960
Enlargement of the Nordic Union Bank head office, Helsinki*
Church center in Wolfsburg, Germany*
Competition entry for cultural center in Leverkusen, Germany
Shopping center in Otaniemi, Espoo*
Power plant at the Pankakoski rapids*
Seinäjoki City Library*

1961
Rovaniemi administrative and cultural center*
Seinäjoki City Theater*
Apartment blocks in Tapiola, Espoo*
Extension to the Stockmann department store, Helsinki
The "Book Palace" (Academic Bookshop) in Helsinki*
Institute of International Education, New York*
Västmanland-Dala student building in Uppsala, Sweden*

1962
Finlandia Hall, Helsinki*
Competition for an extension to the Stockholm Enskilda Bank head
    office in Stockholm, Sweden
Scandinavian House in Reykjavik, Iceland*
Institute of Physical Education, University of Jyväskylä*

1963
Church center in Detmerode, Germany*
Row house in Jakobstad*
Student housing for the University of Technology in
    Otaniemi, Espoo*

1964
Jyväskylä administrative and cultural center*
Master plan for KivenlahtiSoukka, Espoo
Competition entry for British Petroleum administrative building
    in Hamburg, Germany
Competition for the Pohjola Insurance Company head office
    in Helsinki
Schönbühl highrise block in Lucerne, Switzerland*
Office building in Seinäjoki*
Maison Aho, Rovaniemi*
Ekenäs Savings Bank, Ekenäs*
University of Technology library, Otaniemi, Espoo*

1965
William Lehtinen Museum in Helsinki
Administrative building for the Helsinki city power
    company, Helsinki*
Church center in Riola, Italy*
Urban center for Castrop-Rauxel, Germany
Alajärvi center*
Mount Angel Benedictine Abbey library*
Enlargement of the Jyväskylä University gymnasium building*

1966
Concert hall for Siena, Italy
Competition entry for a theater in Wolfsburg, Germany
Housing for Gammelbacka, Porvoo rural municipality
Patricia suburb of Pavia, Italy
Comprehensive exhibition of Aalto's works in Palazzo Strozzi,
    Florence, Italy*

1967
Competition entry for Church center in ZürichAlstetten, Switzerland
Jyväskylä police headquarters*
Villa Kokkonen, Järvenpää*

1968
Water tower for the University of Technology, Otaniemi, Espoo*

1969
Lappia multipurpose building, Rovaniemi*
Museum of Modern Art in Shiraz, Iran
Main church of Lahti*
Villa Skeppet (for Göran Schildt), Ekenäs*
Villa Erica, Monsalieri near Turin, Italy

1971
Alvar Aalto Museum in Jyväskylä*

1973
The Midwest Institute of Scandinavian Culture, Wisconsin, USA

1974
Health spa in Reykjavik, Iceland

1975
Plan for the University of Reykjavik area, Iceland

1978
Commemorative exhibition of Aalto's works in Finlandia Hall,
    Helsinki*

LOCATIONS OF AALTO'S WORKS

A

Aalborg (Denmark), North Jutland Art Museum
Äänekoski, Furnishing of church and parish cafeteria
Alajärvi, Aalto family grave
Alajärvi, "Atrium House"
Alajärvi, Health center
Alajärvi, Mammula
Alajärvi, Municipal hospital
Alajärvi, Renovation of Myllykangas farm
Alajärvi, Parish center
Alajärvi, Shop renovation
Alajärvi, Soldiers' memorial
Alajärvi, Town center
Alajärvi, Town hall
Alajärvi, "Väinölä" house
Alajärvi, "Villa Flora"
Alajärvi, Youth association building, later defense corps building
Anjalankoski, Inkeroinen
Anjalankoski, Bus stations
Anjalankoski, Elementary school
Anjalankoski, Firewood saw mill
Anjalankoski, Garage
Anjalankoski, Housing
Anjalankoski, Kunnila manor
Anjalankoski, Master plan and town plan
Anjalankoski, Officials' club
Anjalankoski, Office building
Anjalankoski, Paper mill
Anjalankoski, Renovation of old industrial installations
Anjalankoski, Saw mill
Anjalankoski, Saunas
Anjalankoski, Semibleached pulp mill
Anjalankoski, Service building for Pasila manor
Anjalankoski, Service buildings
Anjalankoski, Shop in Karhunkangas
Anjalankoski, WAC café
Anttola, Restoration of church
Avesta (Sweden), Johnson Institute
Avesta (Sweden), Master plan
Avesta (Sweden), Skatan district
Avesta (Sweden), Sundh Center
Avesta (Sweden), Town center
Avesta (Sweden), Work for Södra verken plant

B

Baghdad (Iraq), Art museum
Baghdad (Iraq), General post office
Baghdad (Iraq), National Bank, Head office, competition
Bazoches (France), La Maison Carré
Beatenberg (Switzerland), Institute for the International Designers'
        and Architects' Foundation
Beirut (Lebanon), Sabbagh Center
Berlin (Germany), Hansaviertel
Bogskär, Fishermen's housing
Brasilia (Brazil), Finnish Embassy, Furnishing
Bremen (Germany), Neue Vahr High-Rise block

C

Cambridge (Massachusetts, USA), MIT student dormitory
Cambridge (Massachusetts, USA), "Poetry Room"
        at Harvard University
Castrop-Rauxel (Germany), Urban center
Chandraghona (Bangladesh), Paper mill
Copenhagen (Denmark), Glostrup hospital, Competition

D

Darmstadt (Germany), Kranichstein shopping center
Detmerode (Germany), Church center

E

Eau Claire (Wisconsin, USA), The Midwest
        Institute of Scandinavian Culture
Ekenäs, see Tammisaari
Enso, Physician's residence and housing
Enso-Gutzeit, Standard small houses
Enso-Gutzeit, Weekend cottage, Competition
Espoo, Karhusaari and Hanasaari, Town plan and housing
Espoo, KivenlahtiSoukka, Master plan
Espoo, Otaniemi, Garage
Espoo, Otaniemi, Helsinki University of Technology main building
Espoo, Otaniemi, Indoor stadium
Espoo, Otaniemi, Library
Espoo, Otaniemi, Town planning competition and plan
Espoo, Otaniemi, Saunas
Espoo, Otaniemi, Service buildings
Espoo, Otaniemi, Service station
Espoo, Otaniemi, Shopping center, Competition
Espoo, Otaniemi, Shopping center
Espoo, Otaniemi, Student housing
Espoo, Otaniemi, Workshops and laboratories for the Technical
        Research Center of Finland
Espoo, Suvisaaristo, H. Rydgren's summer cottage
Espoo, Tapiola, Apartment blocks
Espoo, Westend, Film studio Erik Blomberg
Essen, Opera and music theater
Eura, Kauttua, Garage
Eura, Kauttua, Housing
Eura, Kauttua, Industrial buildings
Eura, Kauttua, Kindergarten
Eura, Kauttua, Master plan
Eura, Kauttua, Office building
Eura, Kauttua, Sauna

G

Geneva (Switzerland), Palais des Nations, Competition
Gothenburg (Sweden), Drottningtorget, Competition
Gothenburg (Sweden), Municipal offices, Competition

N

Näsijärvi, Villa Kihlman
New York (USA), Furnishing of the Finland House
New York (USA), Institute of International Education
New York (USA), Lincoln Center
New York (USA), Renovation of church
New York (USA), World's Fair pavilion
Noormarkku, Harry Gullichsen's grave
Noormarkku, Health center
Noormarkku, Housing
Noormarkku, Kindergarten
Noormarkku, Outline plan
Noormarkku, Villa Harriet
Noormarkku, Villa Mairea
Nynäshamn, Heimdal housing area
Nynäshamn, Master plan
Nynäshamn, Town hall competition

O

Ohraniemi, Villa and private steamboat
Oulu, Area plan for Typpi company
Oulu, Association and club house for the Toppila company
Oulu, Chemical fertilizer plant for Typpi Oy
Oulu, Conversion of the Laanila office building to an officials' club
Oulu, Bridge
Oulu, Housing for Typpi Oy
Oulu, Merikoski power plant, Competition
Oulu, Plan for University
Oulu, Saunas for Typpi Oy
Oulu, Shop premises
Oulu, Soldiers' memorial, Competition
Oulu, Theater and concert hall
Oulu, Town plan
Oulu, ToppilaVaala pulp mill and office

P

Paimio, Competition entry and implementation
        of tuberculosis sanatorium
Paimio, Housing
Paimio, Sauna
Pamilo, *see* Uimaharju
Pankakoski, Power plant
Paris, World's Fair pavilion
Pärnu (Estonia), Health spa
Pavia (Italy), Patricia suburb
Perniö, Museum
Pertunmaa, Church
Pertunmaa, Renovation of church
Pertunmaa, Hunting lodge
Pietarsaari, *see* Jakobstad
Pihlajavesi, Proposal for renovation of an old people's home
Pori, Pihlava, Area plan for Rieskala
Pori, Pihlava, Houses for Ahlström site managers
Pori, Pihlava, Sauna
Porvoo rural municipality, Gammelbacka suburb
Porvoo rural municipality, Sondby, Villa Eero Manner
Pöytyä, Parish center
Pylkönmäki, Renovation of church

R

Reykjavik (Iceland), Plan for University
Reykjavik (Iceland), Health spa
Reykjavik (Iceland), Scandinavian House
Riola (Italy), Church and parish center
Ristiina, Renovation of church
Rovaniemi, Administrative and cultural center
Rovaniemi, Business and housing complex for Aarne Aho
Rovaniemi, City Library
Rovaniemi, Korkalovaara housing area
Rovaniemi, Korkalovaara, Shopping center
Rovaniemi, Lappia multipurpose building
Rovaniemi, Maison Aho
Rovaniemi, Pirttikoski, Standard houses
Rovaniemi, "Reindeer horn" plan
Rovaniemi, Town hall
Ruotsinpyhtää, Area plan
Ruotsinpyhtää, Housing

S

San Domingo (Dominican Republic), Competition entry
        for a lighthouse
Säynätsalo, Bridge and street lights
Säynätsalo, Commercial building
Säynätsalo, Cultural Center
Säynätsalo, Master plan
Säynätsalo, Municipal offices
Säynätsalo, Old people's home
Säynätsalo, Physican's house
Säynätsalo, Transport stand
Seinäjoki, Bandstand for Defense Corps Building
Seinäjoki, Center plan competitions
Seinäjoki Church parish facilities and vicarage
Seinäjoki, City Library
Seinäjoki, Defense Corps Building
Seinäjoki, Government offices
Seinäjoki, Theater
Seinäjoki, Town hall
Shiraz (Iran), Museum of Modern art
Siena (Italy), Concert hall
Simunankoski fishery
Siuntio, Villa Åke Gartz
Solna (Sweden), Town plan and housing for Huvudsta and Alby
Stockholm (Sweden), Competition for an extension to the
Stockholms Enskilda Bank head office
Stockholm (Sweden), Entry in the ideas competition for renovation
        of the Nedre Norrmalm district
Stockholm (Sweden), Presentation of Karhula glassworks
Stockholm (Sweden), Shop for Interskandinaviska Artek
Stockholm (Sweden), Town plan and housing for
Kampementsbacken in the Gärdet district
Stockholm (Sweden), Villa André
Summa, *see* Vehkalahti
Sunila, *see* Kotka
Suomussalmi, War memorial

T

Tallinn (Estonia), Art Museum, Competition
Tammisaari, Ekenäs Savings Bank
Tammisaari, Villa Skeppet
Tampere, Competition entry for railway station
Tampere, Housing for the Tampella company
Tampere, Second Finnish trade fair
Tampere, Viinikka church, Competition
Tampere, War veterans' village
Tartu (Estonia), Villa Tammekann
Toivakka, Restoration of church
Tornio, Master plan
Torsajärvi, Villa and sauna for Ilmari Luostarinen
Töysä, Terho Manner's house and sauna
Töysä, Soldiers' memorial
Töysä, Vicarage
Turin (Italy), Hotel, congress and office building
Turin (Italy), Prototype warehouse
Turku, Block of rented flats at Uudenmaankatu
Turku, Erik Bryggman's grave
Turku, Choir platform for Turku's 700th anniversary exhibition
Turku, Huonekalutehdas ja Rakennustyötehdas Oy
      furniture company, Annex
Turku, Southwestern Finland Agricultural Cooperative Building
Turku, "Standard apartment block"
Turku, Suomen Biografi cinema
Turku, Turun Sanomat building
Turku, Water tower, Competition
Turku, Unknown assignment for the Crichton & Vulcan shipyard
Turku, Wiklund department store
Turku, 700th anniversary exhibition

U

Uimaharju, Pamilo, Power plant
Uimaharju, Pamilo, Café, kiosk and traffic junction
Uimaharju, Pamilo, Electrician's house
Uppsala (Sweden), VästmannlandDala student building

V

Vaajakoski, Juho Luhta's house
Vaasa, Huutoniemi, Industrial buildings
Vaasa, Huutoniemi, Master plan for Strömberg company
Vaasa, Huutoniemi, Neekerikylä housing area and sauna
Vaasa, Kauppiaitten Osakeyhtiö office block, competition
Vanaja, Housing
Vanaja, Plan for YhteisSisu company
Vantaa, Seutula, Staff housing for Aero Oy
Vantaa, Tikkurila, Competition for Agricultural laboratory
Varkaus, Bleaching plant
Varkaus, Distillery
Varkaus, Foundry
Varkaus, Housing
Varkaus, Indoor market
Varkaus, Invalid's home
Varkaus, Kinkamo, Weekend cabin
Varkaus, Master plan
Varkaus, Minor industrial buildings
Varkaus, Officials' club
Varkaus, Office building
Varkaus, Saunas for A. Ahlström company
Varkaus, Conversion of saw mill
Varkaus, Standard house factory
Vehkalahti, Summa, Garage

Vehkalahti, Summa, Housing
Vehkalahti, Summa, Master plan
Vehkalahti, Summa, Paper mill
Vehkalahti, Summa, Shopping center
Venice (Italy), Finnish Biennale Pavilion
Vienna (Austria), Vogelweidplatz, Competition for a building
      complex for sports concetrs, exhibitions and congresses
Vierumäki, Competition entry for Sports Institute
Viipuri, Competition, later versions and final version of city library
Viipuri, Pirinen house
Viitasaari, Renovation of church

W

Westerstyrskär, Weekend house for Mr. Richmond Temple
Wolfsburg (Germany), Central square, Competition
Wolfsburg (Germany), Church center
Wolfsburg (Germany), Cultural center
Wolfsburg (Germany), Kindergarten
Wolfsburg (Germany), Theater, Competition entry

Z

Zagreb (Yugoslavia), Hospital, Competition
Zürich (Switzerland), Corso Theater restaurant
ZürichAltstetten (Switzerland), Church center and reworked
      plan, Competition

PHOTOGRAPHY CREDITS

All photos are courtesy of Michael Trencher, except the following:

Courtesy of Simo Rista: pages 18, 22, 24, 25, 56–57, 58–59, 60, 61, 72–73, 75, 76–77, 79, 80, 86, 100–101, 103, 108–109, 112–13, 116, 119, 124, 144–45, 205, 206, 207

Courtesy of Michele Merckling: pages 138–39, 140, 184–85

Courtesy of the Alvar Aalto Museum, photographed by M. Kapanen: pages 217, 218, 219, 221, 222–23, 224, 226–27

Courtesy of The Corning Museum of Glass: page 230

All drawings and plans are courtesy of the Alvar Aalto Foundation. Axonometric perspective on page 43 by Antti-Matti Siikala. Axonometric perspective on page 45 by Laura Mark.